2

Extension *for all* through problem solving

Pupil's Textbook

Year 2/Primary 3

Ann Montague-Smith

Paul Harrison

CAMBRIDGE
UNIVERSITY PRESS

CAMBRIDGE UNIVERSITY PRESS
Cambridge, New York, Melbourne, Madrid, Cape Town, Singapore, São Paulo

Cambridge University Press
The Edinburgh Building, Cambridge CB2 2RU, UK

www.cambridge.org
Information on this title: www.cambridge.org/9780521754880

First published 2003
Reprinted 2004, 2006

Printed in Dubai by Oriental Press

A catalogue record for this publication is available from the British Library

ISBN-13 978-0-521-75488-0 paperback
ISBN-10 0-521-75488-7 paperback

Content editing by Beverley Uttley

Cover design by Karen Thomas

Text illustration by Katy Taggart

Project management by Cambridge Publishing Management Limited

The authors and publishers would like to thank schools and individuals who trialled lessons.

KEY TO TEXT
Red text: shows things children need for the activity.
Hint bubbles: give clues to help with the questions.

Contents

1 Frame it!

You need cubes and squared paper.

Use cubes to make an empty square on the grid like this:

Each side is 3 cubes long.

Draw what you have done.

Take your square apart. Make 4 equal lengths.

How many cubes in each length?

How many cubes did you use altogether?

Record what you have done.

Now make a square with sides of 4, then 5, then 6 . . . cubes.

What patterns can you see?

2 Number line

The children in Class 2 made a number line from 1 to 100.

They cut out each digit separately.

To make the number 21, the children cut out a 2 and a 1 .

How many of each digit did they have to cut out to make the number line?

Count all the 1s.
Now what about the 2s?
Now count the 3s.
Can you guess the others?

3 How old is Granny?

Jan and Chris visited their granny.

It was her birthday.

They took her some flowers and a card.

Would you like to know how old I am today?

She gave them five clues. These were:

❶ I am younger than 60 but older than 50.

❷ If you add the digits of my age, you get an even number.

❸ Both of the digits in my age are odd.

❹ The two digits are different.

❺ If you add the digits in my age, you get a 2-digit number that has next-door digits.

Can you work out what the tens digit is? Look carefully at clue number 1.

Now try clue number 2. Which pairs of digits would fit?

Can you work it out?

How old do you think Jan and Chris are?
Make up some clues for their ages for your partner to work out.

4 Number generator

1 Choose any two digits from 1 to 9.

Find all the 2-digit numbers that you can make with these digits.

How many numbers can you make?

2 Choose any three digits from 1 to 9.

Find all the 3-digit numbers that you can make with these digits.

How many numbers can you make?

Is it always this amount of numbers for three digits?

Have you tried making the numbers with digit cards?

Try writing your numbers in order, starting with the lowest.

5 Next-door numbers

Sam and Chris noticed something special about some next-door numbers.

I can make 9 by adding 4 and 5. 4 and 5 are next-door numbers.

$4 + 5 = 9$

$2 + 3 + 4 = 9$

And I can make 9 by adding 2 and 3 and 4. 2, 3 and 4 are next-door numbers.

1 Look at the numbers 1 to 10.

Which numbers can be made using next-door numbers?

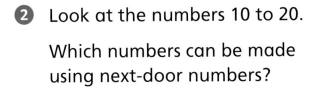

Some numbers can be made in more than one way. Can you find them?

2 Look at the numbers 10 to 20.

Which numbers can be made using next-door numbers?

Which numbers can't be made with next-door numbers?

3 Look at the numbers 20 to 30.

Which numbers can be made using next-door numbers?

6 What's the rule?

Play this game with your partner.

You need a set of number cards.

Try laying out all your number cards in order first.

Choose one of the sorting rules on the stones.
Don't tell your partner which you've chosen!

numbers less than 10

odd numbers

numbers with a 4 in the units place

numbers greater than 20

Put cards that fit the rule into the pond.

Put other cards outside.

Can your partner guess the sorting rule?

Record what you have done.

Now your partner chooses a rule.

Think of your own sorting rule to try.

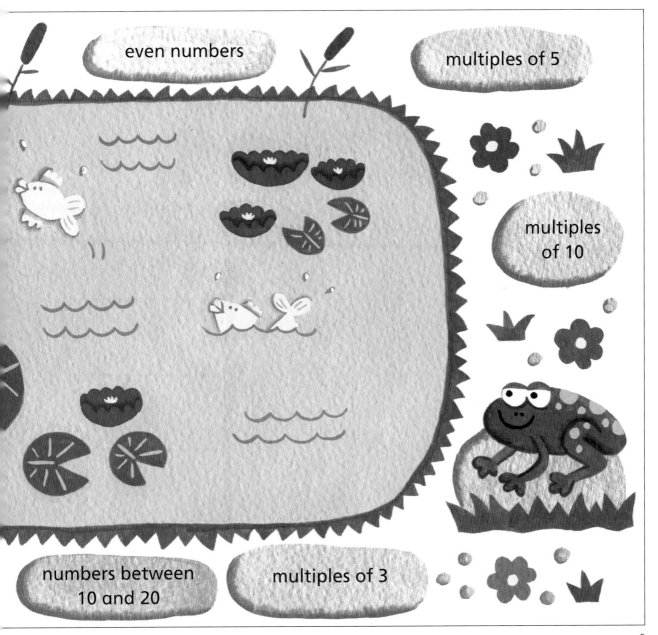

even numbers

multiples of 5

multiples of 10

numbers between 10 and 20

multiples of 3

7 Fraction flags

You need red, blue and green cubes.

Class 2 made some flags for their sports day races.

1 Joe coloured $\frac{1}{2}$ of the squares on his flag red.

Find different ways to do this.

Record your results.

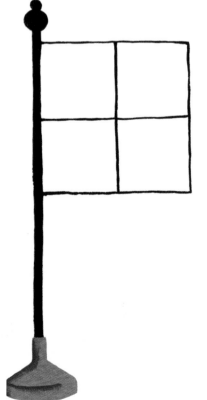

Count out enough cubes to cover $\frac{1}{2}$ of the flag grid.

Use these cubes to make different patterns on the grid.

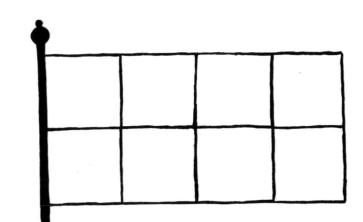

2 Mia coloured $\frac{1}{4}$ of the squares on her flag blue.

Find different ways to do this.

Record your results.

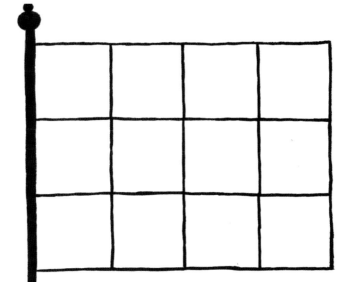

3 Jaz coloured $\frac{1}{3}$ of the squares on his flag green.

Find different ways to do this.

Record your results.

8 Dart totals

You need paper clips.

❶ Use 2 paper clips on the dartboard.

Find a way to make a total of 15.

Write this as a sum.

Now find different ways to make the total 15.

Try this again for totals of 16, 17 and 18.

❷ Use 3 paper clips on the dartboard each time.

Find as many ways of making a total of 20 as you can.

Now choose a total greater than 20. Find as many ways of making it as you can.

Do this again for another number.

What do you notice about your answers?

Record what you have done.

3 Use 3 paper clips on the dartboard each time.

Find as many ways of making a total of 50 as you can.

Now choose a total greater than 50. Find as many ways of making it as you can.

Do this again for another number.

What do you notice about your answers?

Record what you have done. Write about what you have found out.

9 Arithmagons

You need a set of counters with the numbers 1 to 6 on them.

Put a number counter onto each circle. Each side of the triangle must total the centre number.

Can you find more than one way of doing this?

Record your results.

Write about any patterns that you see.

Try writing down
what you try.

10 Four in a row

Play this game with your partner.

You need some counters.

> Take turns to choose 2 numbers from the row of numbers above your grid.
>
> Find the difference between these numbers.
>
> If the answer is on the grid, cover that number with a counter.
>
> The idea of the game is to get 4 counters in a row.

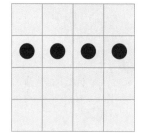 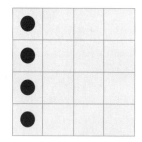 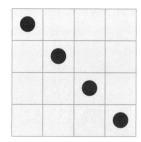 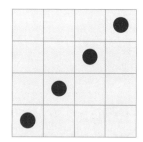

> Choose some different numbers and make another 'Four in a row' game for your friends to play.

Can you find some rules for winning this game?

❶

| 1 | 5 | 8 | 10 | 11 | 12 | 18 | 20 |

4	17	19	10
1	13	7	11
5	15	12	3
2	9	8	6

❷

| 4 | 5 | 7 | 9 | 16 | 19 | 25 |

18	12	2	16
3	10	11	4
6	9	20	15
21	5	14	1

❸

| 14 | 20 | 21 | 34 | 39 | 45 | 50 |

31	14	20	16
24	6	5	25
30	29	18	36
11	7	13	1

11 Square numbers

You need a 100 square and some counters.

1 Look at the pink square on the 100 square.

Add the numbers that are diagonally opposite.

What do you notice?

Why do you think this happens?

Try other squares with 4 numbers in them.

2 Try squares with 9 numbers.

Use smaller numbers.

3 Try squares with 16 numbers.

4 What if the square has 25 numbers in it?

1	2	3	4	5	6	7	8	9	10
11	12	13	14	15	16	17	18	19	20
21	22	23	24	25	26	27	28	29	30
31	32	33	34	35	36	37	38	39	40
41	42	43	44	45	46	47	48	49	50
51	52	53	54	55	56	57	58	59	60
61	62	63	64	65	66	67	68	69	70
71	72	73	74	75	76	77	78	79	80
81	82	83	84	85	86	87	88	89	90
91	92	93	94	95	96	97	98	99	100

Try several squares.

12 Solve it!

You need counters numbered 1 to 9.

Put the counters onto the grid so that the difference between each pair of joined numbers is odd.

Find different ways to do this.

Record your answers on PCM 11.

Write about how you solved it.

Start with one number.

What do you notice about the numbers next to this number?

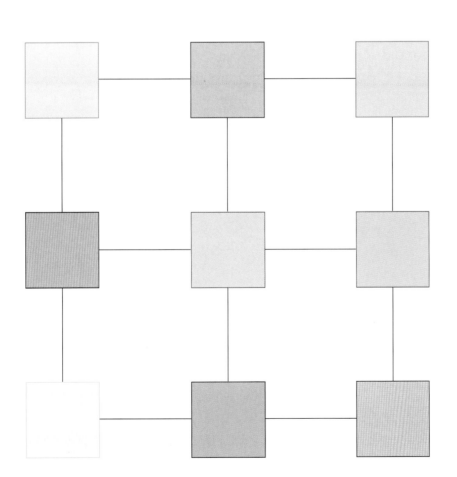

13 Equal totals

You need 16 counters numbered
1, 1, 1, 1, 2, 2, 2, 2, 3, 3, 3, 3, 4, 4, 4, 4.

Put these numbers onto the grid so
that the total of each row, column
and diagonal is the same.

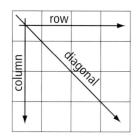

1 This one has been started
for you. Can you complete it?

Which numbers must be:
• in each row?
• in each column?
• in each diagonal?

			3
		2	4
	1	4	2
4	2	3	1

2 Now try this one.

4	3	2	1
2	1		3
3			2
			4

Use PCM 12 and try some
of your own.

14 Make fifteen

Play this game with your partner.

You need digit cards 1, 2, 3, 4, 5, 6, 7, 8 and 9.

Put the cards in a line, in order.

Take turns to take a card.

Keep taking cards until one of you has three cards that total 15.

This wins the game.

Can you find a way of winning each time?

What if you go first?

What different ways can you make totals of 15 with just three cards?

Use the number line to check your totals.

Mmm. 6 + 7 = 13. What card do I need to make 15?

| 0 | 1 | 2 | 3 | 4 | 5 | 6 | 7 | 8 | 9 | 10 | 11 | 12 | 13 | 14 | 15 |

15 Counter shapes

You need some counters.

1 Count out 12 counters.

Put some of your counters onto the grid to make a rectangle.

Which numbers of counters will make rectangles?

2 Count out 20 counters.

Put 10 of your counters onto the grid to make a rectangle.

Try making rectangles with other numbers of counters.

Which numbers will make more than one rectangle?

Investigate numbers bigger than 10.

3 Count out 30 counters.

Put 20 of your counters onto the grid to make a rectangle. Record your array.

Try making rectangles with other numbers of counters.

Which numbers make more than one rectangle?

Investigate numbers larger than 20.

Try a small number of counters first. Now try adding one more counter, and one more again.

Which numbers make a square?

Record what you find.

16 Two-dice totals

Investigate this puzzle with your partner.

Take turns to roll 2 dice.

Add the dice scores to find the total.

Cover the total on the grid.
Can you cover all of the numbers?

Can you cover some numbers more
than once?

Which numbers can be made in different ways with 2 dice?

Which numbers can
you make in different ways?

Which numbers can be made
in only one way?

1	2	3
4	5	6
7	8	9
10	11	12

17 Animal quackers

The farmer has some cows and some ducks in a field.

He counts their legs. There are 32 legs altogether.

How many cows and how many ducks are there?

Find different answers.

Stuck?
What if there were
just 8 legs? Or 12?

Try different numbers of legs.

Suppose there were 10 legs, what then?

What patterns can you see in your answers?

18 Digits

Look at this picture of Tom.

How many fingers does Tom have?

How many toes?

How many fingers and toes altogether?

Now look at this picture of Tom and Holly.

How many fingers do they have?

How many toes?

How many fingers and toes altogether?

What if there were 3 children?

How many fingers?

How many toes?

How many fingers and toes altogether?

Now try for 4, 5, 6 . . . children.

What pattern can you see?

Write about it.

19 Pocket money

Every Saturday, Grandad gives Josh some coins as pocket money.

Grandad makes sure that all of the coins are different.

1 Grandad gives Josh 3 coins.

He chooses these from 10p, 20p, 50p and £1 coins.

Investigate how much money Josh could have.

Put out all the possible coins.

Put them in order.

2 Grandad gives Josh 4 coins chosen from 10p, 20p, 50p, £1 and £2 coins.

Investigate how much money Josh could have.

3 Grandad gives Josh 5 coins.

None of the coins are copper.

Investigate how much money Josh could have.

20 Leapfrog

There are 2 frogs by the pond.

One is called Grunt and the other is called Croak.

In the pond, 30 stepping stones go from one side to the other.

1 Grunt says 'I shall jump 2 stepping stones at a time'.

Croak says 'I shall jump 5 stepping stones at a time'.

Which stepping stones will they each land on?

2 Grunt says 'I shall jump 2 stepping stones at a time'.

Croak says 'I shall jump 3 stepping stones at a time'.

Which stepping stones will they each land on?

Which stepping stones will not be visited?

3 Grunt says 'I shall jump 3 stepping stones at a time'.

Croak says 'I shall jump 4 stepping stones at a time'.

Which stepping stones will they each land on?

Which stepping stones will not be visited?

Write some sentences to explain your results.

Use PCM 13.

Draw in Grunt's path across the stepping stones.

Now draw in Croak's path.

21 Make a shape

Make a screen between you and your partner.

One of you make a shape from the shape tiles.

Now describe the shape you have made to your partner.

Can your partner make the same shape?

These words may help you.

top   bottom   side

between   opposite

corner   left   next to

right   edge   beside

centre   below   above   over   underneath   under   middle

Listen carefully to
your partner.

Put each shape where you are told.

Do just one piece
at a time.

22 Shape pairs

Cut out the shapes on PCM 16.

Fit pairs together to make this shape.

Hmm. These 2 don't fit.

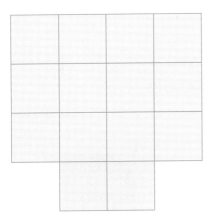

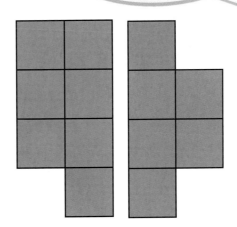

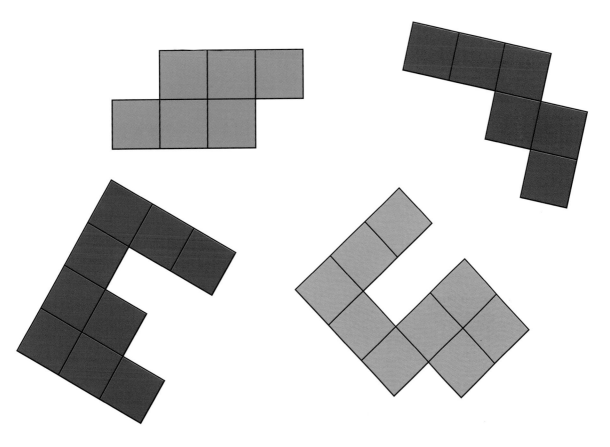

23 Cube shapes

Use 4 cubes each time.

Make different shapes.

It is possible to make 8 different shapes.

Can you find them all?

Which shapes will lie flat on the table, with no cubes in the air?

Draw the shapes that will lie flat.

How could you draw shapes that will not lie flat?

Make sure that each shape you make is different.

Turn the shapes you make to check.

24 Four-sided shapes

You need 2 of each shape.

Choose 2 shape tiles.

Put them side by side.

How many different 4-sided shapes can you make?

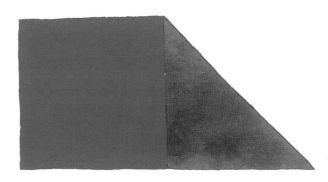

Sketch your results.

Now try with different tiles.

25 Four the same

You need 16 cubes.

1 Make 4 shapes like this:

Each shape must be a different colour.

Cover the grid with your shapes. Draw what you have done.
Try each of these shapes. Will they all fit?

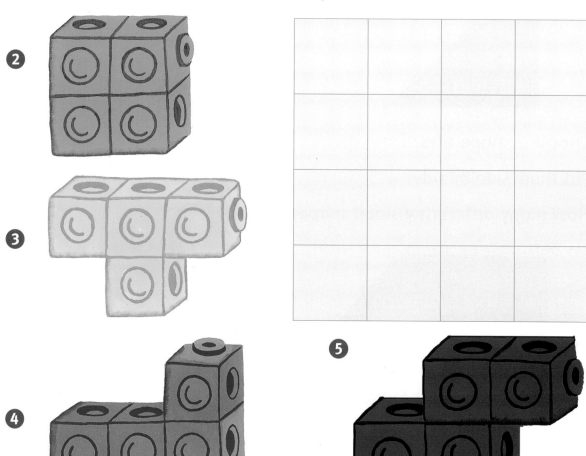

26 Triangle trap

You need a pin board and some elastic bands.

Make some triangles on the pin board.

Find some triangles that will trap 1 pin.

Now find triangles that will trap 2 pins,
3 pins, 4 pins . . .

Can you find a triangle with no pins trapped?

Try different-shaped triangles.

What happens if you try a right-angled triangle?

27 Favourite TV programmes

Sum Ying was going to see her grandma on Saturday.

She decided to record her favourite programmes for that day.

Sum Ying can't watch TV after 9:00 pm.

❶ The videotape will take 1 hour of programmes.

Decide what to record.

Try to fill as much of the tape as you can.

❷ The videotape will take 2 hours of programmes.

Decide what to record.

Try to fill as much of the tape as you can.

❸ The videotape will take 3 hours of programmes.

Decide what to record.

Try to fill as much of the tape as you can.

Saturday T.V. guide

News 1		9:00 am
Cartoons 1	★	9:15 am
Film: Adventure on Treasure Island		9:30 am
Cartoons 2		10:30 am
Film: A Space Adventure	♫	12:00 noon
News 2		1:00 pm
Cartoons 3		1:15 pm
Film: The School Play	★	1:30 pm
Cartoons 4		2:30 pm
Blue Peter Saturday Special		3:00 pm
Top of the Pops		3:45 pm
Cartoons 5	★	4:15 pm
Cartoons 6		4:45 pm
Sports results	♫	5:30 pm
Generation Game		6:00 pm
Dog Eat Dog		7:00 pm
Lottery results		7:45 pm
Casualty	★	8:00 pm
Football results		8:45 pm
News 3		9:00 pm

28 Ticker timer

You need a coffee jar lid, some Plasticine, a piece of card, sticky tape, ruler and scissors.

Make a ticker timer.

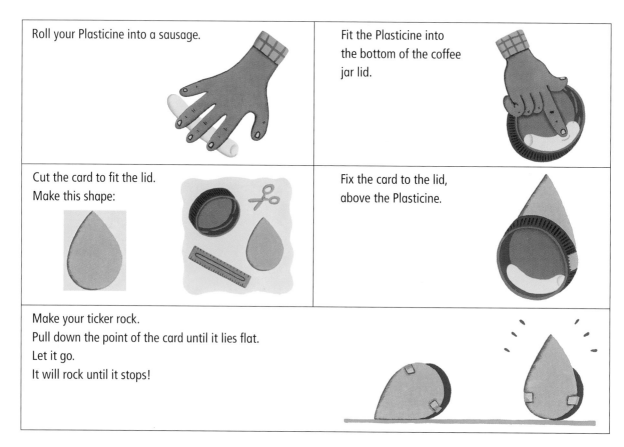

Roll your Plasticine into a sausage.

Fit the Plasticine into the bottom of the coffee jar lid.

Cut the card to fit the lid. Make this shape:

Fix the card to the lid, above the Plasticine.

Make your ticker rock.
Pull down the point of the card until it lies flat.
Let it go.
It will rock until it stops!

Find out how long your ticker rocks for.

Use your ticker timer to measure:
- how many times you can write your name
- how many numbers, in order, you can write
- how many times you can draw a neat square

What else could you do in the time that your ticker rocks?

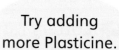

Try adding more Plasticine.

29 Sand weight challenge

This is a special weighing and balancing challenge.

You need some sand, small bags,
bag ties, labels, several 20 g and 50 g weights
and a 2-pan balance.

Try to make bags of sand that weigh:

1. 20 g
2. 40 g
3. 50 g
4. 100 g
5. 10 g
6. 30 g
7. 60 g
8. 70 g
9. 80 g
10. 90 g

What weights can you make with 50 g and 20 g?

Try making a list.

Remember, you can only use your 20 g and 50 g weights to help you each time.

Hmm . . . How can you make 10 g using 20 g weights?

30 Hoop roll

Sam and Shefali are rolling hoops along the playground.

Investigate how far a hoop will roll in one turn.

Glossary

array

A collection ordered in columns and rows.

column

A **column** in a grid goes from top to bottom in a straight line.

The numbers 3, 4, 5, 6 and 7 are in a column.

		3		
		4		
		5		
		6		
		7		

diagonal

A **diagonal** in a grid goes from the top left corner to the bottom right corner, or from the top right corner to the bottom left corner in a straight line.

The numbers 1, 2, 3, 4 and 5 are in a diagonal.

The numbers 9, 8, 3, 7 and 6 are in a diagonal.

difference

The **difference** between two numbers is the amount that one number is greater or less than the other number.

8 is 3 greater than 5.

3 is 5 less than 8.

digit

A **digit** is a number symbol. The digits we use are 0, 1, 2, 3, 4, 5, 6, 7, 8 and 9. All of our other numbers are made from these digits.

27 has the digit 2 in the tens place, and the digit 7 in the units place.

We also use the word 'digits' to mean our fingers, thumbs and toes.

empty number line

An **empty number line** can be used to help with addition or subtraction.

For 36 + 28

36 + 28 = 36 + 20 + 4 + 4

For 73 − 27

73 − 27 = 73 − 20 − 3 − 4

even numbers

An **even number** can be divided exactly by 2. For example, 6 ÷ 2 = 3

All even numbers end in either 0, 2, 4, 6 or 8. So 358 is an even number.

fraction

A fraction is another way to divide a number. Half of 6 is 3.

Shapes can also be divided into equal parts, called fractions.

$\frac{1}{2}$ of 6 is 3

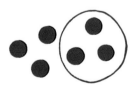

gram

This is a unit for measuring weight.

1000 **grams** make a kilogram.

grid

A **grid** is made from lines going across and down to form squares. It usually makes a large square or rectangle shape.

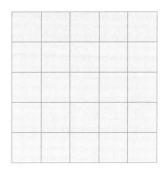

hexagon

A **hexagon** is a flat shape with 6 sides.

multiple

If you start at 0 and count in equal steps, then all the numbers in that sequence are **multiples** of that step.

0, 2, 4, 6 and 8 … are all multiples of 2.

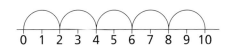

next-door numbers

These numbers are also called **consecutive numbers**. This means that they are next to each other in order. So: 3 and 4 are consecutive numbers, or **next-door numbers**.

number line

A **number line** shows the counting numbers in order. It often starts at 0, but it can begin with any counting number.

0 1 2 3 4 5 6 7 8 9 10 11 12 13 14 15 16 17 18 19 20 21 22 23 24 25 26 27 28 29 30

odd numbers

An **odd number** cannot be divided exactly by 2. For example, 7 divided by 2 is 3, with 1 left over.

Odd numbers end in either 1, 3, 5, 7 or 9. So 423 is an odd number.

octagon

An **octagon** is a flat shape with 8 sides.

pentagon

A **pentagon** is a flat shape with 5 sides.

pin board

A **pin board** has pegs on it; they usually make squares. You can fit elastic bands onto the pegs to make patterns. It is sometimes called a **geoboard**.

quadrilateral

A **quadrilateral** is any flat shape that has 4 sides.

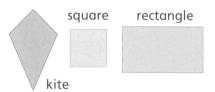

square   rectangle

kite

All of these shapes are quadrilaterals.

rectangle

A **rectangle** is a 4-sided flat shape that has 4 right angles. Its opposite sides are the same length.

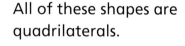

right angle

A **right angle** is a $\frac{1}{4}$ turn.

To make a right angle tester, fold a piece of paper in half and then in half again.

row

A **row** in a grid goes from side to side in a straight line.

The numbers 3, 4, 5, 6 and 7 are in a row.

3	4	5	6	7

square

A **square** is a flat shape that has 4 right angles and 4 sides the same length.

tally

A **tally** is where we make marks to show the number counted.

total

Total means how many there are altogether. It is the sum found by adding.

5 + 6 = 11

11 is the total of 5 and 6.

triangle

A **triangle** is a flat shape with 3 sides and 3 angles.

These are all triangles.

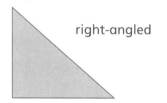
right-angled

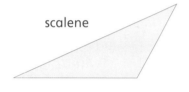
scalene

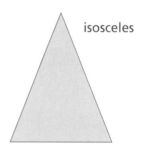
isosceles

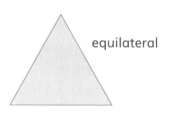
equilateral

FIRST STEPS

TO

BALLROOM

DANCING

by
Lyndon B Wainwright

Lyric Books Limited

© 1993 Lyric Books Limited
Central House, 7-8 Ritz Parade, Western Avenue, London W5 3RA, England

Text Copyright © 1993 Lyndon B Wainwright

First published in 1993
Reprinted in 1994

ISBN 0 7111 0089 6

Printed in Belgium by Proost International Book Production

Photography by John Spragg

Our thanks to Imperial College Dance Club, London
for their help and especially to the dancers who were
photographed for this book:

Sonia Abubacker, Zoe Antoniou, Bryan Crotax, Patricia Domnesteanu,
Satin Gungah, Alice Jacques, Alexander Kurniawan,
Andrew Smith, Joanne Wade.

Contents

Introduction

Ballroom Dancing is a social grace. It is an entertainment and a pastime. It is a sport and exercise. Above all it is fun.

Ballroom Dancing is for all ages. While it is a game for children, for their parents it was and remains a means to meet socially and court for life. For the elderly it is light exercise, a way of keeping trim and a way to foster memories of youth. There is no time for retirement.

Being able to dance is a social asset for life.

Ballroom Dancing is an entertainment. Millions go to dance classes. Millions go to dance halls and millions watch both amateur and professional Ballroom Dancing competitions on television. At schools and Universities the Ballroom Dancing Clubs are social focal points for pleasure and competition. Ballroom Dancing will soon be an Olympic sport.

This book is a simple guide to the first steps in Ballroom Dancing. It includes the most popular dances at social functions ... at that Dinner Dance or Ball where you want to take the floor without embarrassment. Dances such as the Waltz and Quickstep are relaxing and romantic. The Jive, the Samba and the Cha Cha Cha are lively and pulsating. They are all an expression of partnership with couples moving in time to music.

Why learn from a book? A book is an introduction to learn enough to venture to Ballroom Dancing classes. It is for reference before a competition. Nothing can replace the teacher. Nothing can replace the feel of a practised partner.

Learning is fun. Do not be bashful. Move, laugh and smile even at your mistakes. You will gain confidence and with confidence comes bravado. With bravado will come style and elegance that others will envy.

This book is to inspire.

How To Learn

Keeping it simple

In this book we aim to give a simple introduction to the most popular dances, without intricate details or the finer points of techniques. If you decide to pursue dancing further a good teacher can soon introduce you to more advanced movements.

Fashions in clothes change but it is worth saying that both ladies and gentlemen should wear light shoes and that for most dances the ladies will find it easier if they have a heel to their shoe rather than a flat shoe.

You will all have seen expert dancers performing on the television and it may be that in years to come you will aspire to those giddy heights. However, we are concerned with learning the basics of social dancing; and fortunately there is just as much enjoyment in dancing for the beginner as there is for the more advanced and experienced dancer.

The Dances

There are two sorts of dance included in this book. The first are called contact dances in which the man takes hold of the lady and holds her close to him throughout. This is the hold used for the waltz, quickstep and foxtrot and we will describe it later. The other sort of dance is that in which the man holds the lady, but at some little distance away from him. In this category are the cha cha cha, rumba and jive.

The Music

Before you start any dance you will need to know what the appropriate dance is for the music being played. This is dictated by the rhythm of the music and the speed at which it is played (called the **tempo**). There are exceptions but most of the tunes to which you will dance are written with four beats to the bar or with three beats to the bar. Examples of music written in four beats to the bar (4/4 or **common time**) are 'Dancing in the Rain', 'If you knew Susie', 'As Time Goes By' and 'The Way we Were'. Music in 3/4 time is invariably that of waltzes such as 'Beautiful Dreamer', 'Scarborough Fair' and so on.

The commonest music of all is that written in 4/4 time and here the beginner is lucky because to this music there is one dance which can be used in all circumstances. We call it social foxtrot and not only is it suitable for most music in 4/4 time, whether it be fairly quick or very slow, but it is also suitable for dancing in crowded conditions such as the traditional cafe or club dance floor.

The Closed Hold

Before we start learning the dance itself, let us consider how the couple should stand. Both man and lady should stand up and avoid slouching. The normal hold for the waltz, social foxtrot and quickstep is called the **closed hold**. For this, the lady stands close to the man and a tiny fraction to her left. The man places his hand on the lady's back just below the shoulder blade and holds the lady's right hand comfortably in his left hand somewhere level with his chin, with the elbow held slightly away from the body at a comfortable angle. This hold is much more casual than that you will see better dancers use, but we suggest you do not try anything more elaborate at the start.

Leading

It is quite natural for beginners to worry about whether they are going to tread on their partner's feet. The man's ability to 'lead' is important and, provided you stand up well and keep contact between you and your partner's body, leading is more a question of confidence than any special ability.

If you wish to step forward with your left foot it is necessary for you first to settle your weight firmly on your right foot. Let us try a little exercise. Stand with your feet five to seven centimetres (two or three inches) apart with your weight felt equally between both feet. Sway the weight over to the right foot until you feel the left foot free of the floor. You are now ready to move the left foot forward, side or back. If you have hold of a partner and do exactly the same as we have just done, your partner should also feel your weight settle over to your right, that is her left, and she should allow her weight to move with yours. This will leave her right foot free to move when you use your left foot.

Now if you move off in the direction in which you wish to go, making sure that the body moves with the foot and that you do not stick out the foot first and then follow with the body, your partner will be compelled to move in the corresponding direction. However, until you have a good deal of experience do not take steps which are too long. Restrict yourselves to steps which are shorter than those you would use when walking, although they have the same character as walking steps.

Equally important is the lady's ability to follow her partner's lead. The man leads the lady with his body and by means of the distribution of weight. So, the lady must respond to the way the man settles his weight onto one side or the other before moving off. Try not to fight the man as he settles his weight - go with him. He can move off in any direction and again as his body pushes you back or sideways, relax and go along with the thrust of his body. Should he move backwards he will keep a firm hold on your back with his right hand and you will feel the pressure pulling you forward. Try not to resist. Above all, avoid trying to take over the lead, even if your partner gets his steps confused, as this could turn an enjoyable dance into a wrestling match!

This is the basis of leading and following in all contact dances. Once you are moving it is important to take the weight fully on each step in turn and not to try to rush matters. This is another reason for keeping the steps quite short. You need to be quite expert before you can stride out with the length of step used by experienced dancers.

What is a Step?

Throughout this book we write about **steps** and dancers use two meanings for the word step.

Correctly, a **step** is the movement of one foot from one position to its next position. However, groups of steps such as the six steps of the right turn (or natural turn) in the waltz, are often called **steps** instead of the more correct term **figure**.

We need to think a little about individual steps and, in particular, backward steps. We are all used to walking forward and forward steps in dancing do not differ much from walking. However, moving backwards is something for which most of us have little practice.

Particularly in the dances where man and lady stand with body contact (such as waltz and quickstep) some attention needs to be given to how backward steps should be taken.

Consider what happens when you step backwards with the right foot. If you start with the full weight over the left foot, this should make it possible to swing the right foot forward or back. When stepping back with the right foot the weight is kept on the left foot while the right leg is swung backwards. As the right foot moves backwards, the right ankle should be straightened so that the right toes are pushed backwards. If someone stands behind you as you step back he should see the sole of your right shoe.

How To Learn

It also gets the toes back out of harm's way and ensures that you will not get your toes trodden on. The hips and body weight are held over the supporting foot as long as possible - in this case the left foot.

When the back foot reaches the position it is to move to it acts as a spring to control the pace at which the weight is moved from the front foot and on to it.

It is very helpful if the foot is flexible, for this will assist in avoiding a sudden fall backwards of the weight on to the back foot. The back foot acts as a shock absorber and smooths out backwards movement.

Although both man and lady need to think about back steps it is more important for the lady, since a good use of the back foot helps her to follow the lead of the man.

Following Descriptions

When steps are given in various **figures** the instruction will be to **step forward** or **step back** or **step to side**. There is nothing difficult about these instructions but one little point needs to be explained.

Stand facing the nearest wall with the weight felt on the right foot. Now **step to side** with the left foot. This will leave you with your feet apart and both feet the same distance from the wall. This is the position you will reach at the end of all steps taken to the side, no matter what has gone before. In other words, the step taken to the side is moved to a position to the side of the supporting foot.

Try this same action now after you have taken a forward step. Again face towards the nearest wall and take a step forward with the right foot. At the end of this step the right foot is in front of the left foot just as at the end of one walking step. If from this position I ask you to **step to side** with left foot, the left foot is moved to a position level with the right foot (the same distance from the wall) and about half a metre (one and a half feet) to the side.

The position which you have reached is the same as if you had started with the feet together before the side step was taken. What you should not do at the end of a forward step if then stepping to the side is merely to move the foot sideways without bringing it up level with the supporting foot. This latter movement is awkward but sometimes beginners get confused about the action of side steps.

Each instruction given for the dances in this book describes the position reached at the end of one step.

More about the Music

As we have mentioned, the music dictates the dance you are going to perform. Each dance has its own characteristic music and we have to set down the amount of music taken up by each step of each figure.

Any way of counting this - which we call the **rhythm** - which conveys what is needed is acceptable; 'yackity yak' would be quite adequate. However, so that you know how long each step should take we must go into more detail.

Waltz music has three beats to the bar, and the first is emphasised by the band. If you listen to good waltz music you should not find it difficult to pick out this stronger beat. You can then count the music 'one, two, three' and so on. The simple waltz figures are counted in this way.

Sometimes four steps are fitted into one bar of waltz music and this can be done in many ways, though in the simpler figures it is done by taking two steps in the time normally occupied by the second beat of music. When this happens instead of counting 'one, two, three' we count 'one, two and three' in order to fit the four counts into three beats the count of 'two and' are hurried so that each only occupies half of one beat. The beat value for each step is then:- one, half, half, one.

In dances written in 4/4 time, that is four beats to the bar, the emphasised beats are, in foxtrot and quickstep, the first and third. They are not so strongly emphasised as the waltz first beat but nevertheless can be heard if you listen carefully. In such dances we have commonly two sorts of steps in the figures. One type is a slow step which takes up two beats and the other is a quick step which takes up one beat. It would be possible for you to have four quick steps in a bar and in more advanced dancing this is quite usual but, for a little while, you will always find that your quick steps are interspersed with slow ones. The bars of music in 4/4 time for beginners are usually either 'slow, slow' or 'slow, quick quick' or 'quick, quick, slow'.

Can you think of the tune of Jingle Bells? The words Jingle Bells near the start of the music occupy one bar of music. You will remember that the words are repeated twice; 'Jingle Bells, Jingle Bells'. This is two bars of music and represents a rhythm of 'quick, quick, slow, quick, quick, slow'. In this case 'Jin' is equivalent to 'quick', 'gle' is equivalent to 'quick', 'bells' is equivalent to 'slow'. For those of you who understand music we print these two bars below, together with the appropriate count for dancing to them.

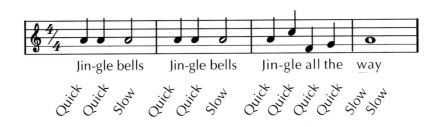

This use of Jingle Bells as an illustration is merely to help you understand how long quick and slow steps take. In practice slow and quick steps do not have to fit precisely to melodic lines, but have merely to fit to the bars of music.

Until you have a good deal of experience slow steps will always start on either the first or third beat of the bar and never on the second or fourth beat and you will always have quick steps coming in pairs and not singly.

Joining Figures Together

Dances consist of individual figures, as described in this book, joined together one after another. In the cha cha cha and rumba this is simple, for all figures, at the level covered by this book, can follow each other in any sequence.

In most other dances the man has the responsibility of selecting one figure after another, joining them together to form a continuous sequence.

This is largely a matter of experience, but I will be giving groupings of figures in each dance at appropriate points in the text.

First Steps - Social Foxtrot

Introduction

The first dance to learn is the social foxtrot. There are many reasons for this, but perhaps the most important is that this is the dance you will find throughout the world.

It can be done to a variety of types of music, it needs very little space, and it is probably the world's commonest dance. Wherever you may go this is a dance you will be able to perform and which your partner will be able to follow.

It can be danced to any music written in 4/4 time, that is to say music with four beats or accents per bar. Musicians sometimes call this **common time**.

First we will learn the basic movement. I will explain this in two stages, first without any turn and then adding a little turn to it.

If you are fortunate enough to be learning with a partner, start by facing each other with your hands resting lightly on each other's shoulders. This will enable both of you to see how your steps fit with your partner's. If you do not have a partner, it is not a bad idea to hold the book in both hands in front of you and to regard the book as your partner.

The man starts facing the nearest wall but a metre or two away from it, while the lady stands in front of and facing the man so that she has her back towards the nearest wall.

Basic Movement

Man's Steps

1.	Right foot forward	Slow
2.	Left foot to side	Quick
3.	Right foot closes to left foot	Quick
4.	Left foot back	Slow
5.	Right foot back	Slow
6.	Left foot to side	Quick
7.	Right foot closes to left foot	Quick
8.	Left foot forward	Slow

Lady's Steps

1.	Left foot back	Slow
2.	Right foot to side	Quick
3.	Left foot closes to right foot	Quick
4.	Right foot forward	Slow
5.	Left foot forward	Slow
6.	Right foot to side	Quick
7.	Left foot closes to right foot	Quick
8.	Right foot back	Slow

Social Foxtrot

MAN Basic movement

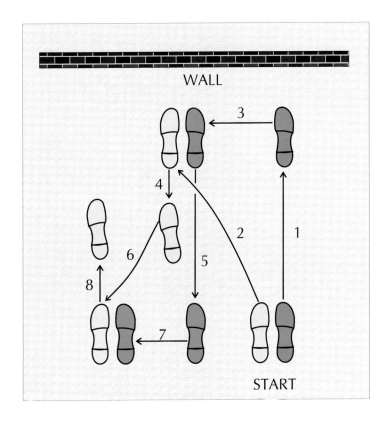

Social Foxtrot

LADY Basic movement

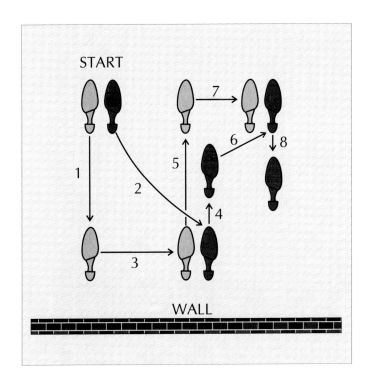

First Steps - Social Foxtrot

When you are sure you have mastered the steps of the basic movement take hold of your partner in the **closed hold** described in the section **About Learning** and try what you have learnt so far.

Basic Movement with Turn
(Quarter Turns)

We are now going to use the same basic movement but add to it a little turn. On steps 1,2 and 3 there is a little turn to the right - more about this in a moment - on step 4 there is no turn whilst on steps 5,6 and 7 there is a little turn to the left. No turn on step 8.

Quarter Turns

Man's Steps with Turn

1.	*Right foot forward, starting to turn to right.*	*Slow*
2.	*Left foot to side, still turning to right.*	*Quick*
3.	*Right foot closes to left foot, still turning to right so that the man is now facing straight towards the wall.*	*Quick*
4.	*Left foot back.*	*Slow*
5.	*Right foot back, starting to turn to left.*	*Slow*
6.	*Left foot to side, still turning to left.*	*Quick*
7.	*Right foot closes to left foot, still turning to left so that the man is now again facing slanting towards the wall.*	*Quick*
8.	*Left foot forward.*	*Slow*

Lady's Steps with Turn

1.	*Left foot back, starting to turn to right.*	*Slow*
2.	*Right foot to side, still turning to right.*	*Quick*
3.	*Left foot closes to right foot, still turning to right, so that lady now has her back to the nearest wall.*	*Quick*
4.	*Right foot forward.*	*Slow*
5.	*Left foot forward, starting to turn to left.*	*Slow*
6.	*Right foot to side, still turning to left.*	*Quick*
7.	*Left foot closes to right foot, still turning to left, so that lady is now backing in a slanting direction to the nearest wall.*	*Quick*
8.	*Right foot back.*	*Slow*

First Steps - Social Foxtrot

Because we are turning we do not start facing straight towards the wall. If the man will face the nearest wall and turn a little to his left so that he is now looking slanting at the wall (about 45 degrees for those mathematically inclined) this is the correct starting direction. The lady again faces the man and she will now have her back to the wall in a slanting direction. The man has made just a little turn; first to the right and then to the left.

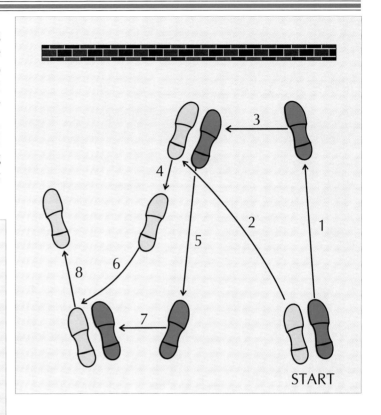

Social Foxtrot
MAN Quarter turns

TIPS

Sometimes pupils get confused about which is a right turn and which is a left turn. Shall we check?

If you face the wall and place some object on your right hand side and turn your body the shortest way so that you are able to look at the object, then you have turned to the right. This can happen while you are stepping forward, back-wards or sideways and is always a right turn irrespective of the direction of the step.

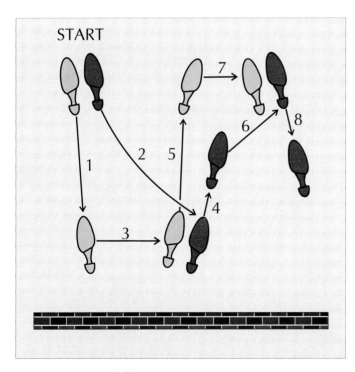

Social Foxtrot
LADY Quarter turns

Now let us go through the lady's steps for this figure with turn.

I have described this figure with one eighth of a turn to right, followed by one eighth of a turn to left. More turn, up to a quarter can be made, hence the name 'Quarter Turns'.

When you have completed the whole basic movement then it can be repeated so that,when the man finishes the movement by stepping forward on his left foot, it leaves him ready to step forward again with the right foot for step 1 of the same figure. The figure when repeated will take you along the room, the general direction of the figure remaining parallel to the wall.

What on earth to do when you come to a corner?

Corners are not so much of a problem as

you might imagine. Absolute beginners can move around a corner just using the basic movement.

All you need to do is to dance the first half of the basic movement without turn, but then turn to the left on the second half. These four steps are numbers 5 to 8 of the **quarter turns.** If you repeat this grouping twice it will take you round the corner and you will be ready to move along the next wall.

Another way of negotiating a corner is to use the right turn. Dancers often call right turns **natural turns** and similarly left turns **reverse turns**. You will come across these names later on. For the moment think only of this as the right turn. The right turn is made by taking the first four steps of the basic movement with turn to the right and then repeating these four steps.

Right Turn

Man's Steps

1.	*Right foot forward, turning body to right.*	*Slow*
2.	*Left foot to side, still turning to right.*	*Quick*
3.	*Right foot closes to left foot, still turning to right.*	*Quick*
4.	*Left foot back, still turning to right.*	*Slow*
5.	*Right foot is now forward in front of body and the weight is changed forward from the left foot and on to the right, still turning to right.*	*Slow*
6.	*Left foot to side, still turning to right.*	*Quick*
7.	*Right foot closes to left foot.*	*Quick*
8.	*Left foot back.*	*Slow*

Lady's Steps

1.	*Left foot back, turning to right.*	*Slow*
2.	*Right foot to side, still turning to right.*	*Quick*
3.	*Left foot closes to right foot, still turning to right.*	*Quick*
4.	*Right foot forward, still turning to right.*	*Slow*
5.	*Left foot a very small step back, still turning to right.*	*Slow*
6.	*Right foot to side, still turning to right.*	*Quick*
7.	*Left foot closes to right foot, still turning to right.*	*Quick*
8.	*Right foot forward*	*Slow*

First Steps - Social Foxtrot

TIP

It is possible to make quite a lot of turn to the right on these eight steps but to start with take it easy and do not try to make too much.

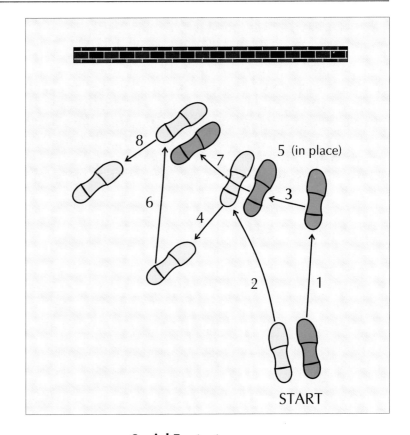

Social Foxtrot
MAN Right turn

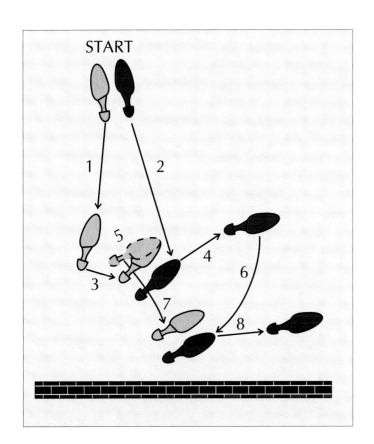

Social Foxtrot
LADY Right turn

First Steps - Social Foxtrot

The right turn, like the basic movement, can be repeated and it is possible to remain more or less on one spot on the floor and continue repeating the figure until you have turned fully round and are facing in the direction in which you started.

At a corner it is possible to do the figure turning to the right until you are facing towards the next wall at the end of the figure.

You now have two figures, the **basic movement**, with or without turn, and the **right turn**. At this stage in your lessons you must always do enough right turns to finish facing the nearest wall. Provided you do this it is then possible to follow the right turn with more right turns or with the basic movement. Of course it is also possible to follow the basic movement with a set of right turns.

As a guide, you should aim to complete one turn in four or less 'right turns'.

Social Foxtrot Step 5 Quarter Turns

Social Foxtrot Hold

First Steps - Cha Cha Cha

Introduction

You have learnt a little social foxtrot so now is the time to learn just one grouping in the popular cha cha cha. The music is sure to be with us for some time to come, for many modern tunes are written with this rhythm. It is written with four beats to the bar. What differentiates the cha cha cha from other music written with four beats to the bar is that there is a little rhythmic triplet joining each bar to the next.

One bar of music can be counted for the purpose of the dance 'one, two, three, four, and'. If counted in this way the counts 'four, and' fit in the time usually taken up by the count 'four' alone; that is to say they are half the time they would normally take. Two bars of music would be counted: 'one, two, three, four, and, one, two, three, four, and'.

The heavy beat is the one played at the beginning of the bar and counted 'one'. The counts at the end of the bar 'four, and' plus the first count of the next bar, the count 'one', make a little group or triplet - the 'cha cha cha'.

It is this triplet which gives the cha cha cha much of its special sound.

In all the simple figures every time there is a 'cha cha cha' count there is a little group of three steps called a **chasse**. There are two main chasses, one starting with the left and one with the right foot. Let us learn these first.

Step 3 of Cha Cha Cha Chasse to Left

First Steps - Cha Cha Cha

Cha Cha Cha Chasse to Left

Man's Steps

1.	Left foot small step to side	cha
2.	Right foot half closes to left foot	cha
3.	Left foot small step to side	Cha

(small 'c' indicates half a beat whilst capital 'C' shows that the step takes a full beat).

Lady's Steps

1.	Right foot small step to side	cha
2.	Left foot half closes to right foot	cha
3.	Right foot small step to side	Cha

(small 'c' indicates half a beat whilst capital 'C' shows that the step takes a full beat).

Cha Cha Cha Chasse to Right

Man's Steps

1.	Right foot small step to side	cha
2.	Left foot half closes to right foot	cha
3.	Right foot small step to side	Cha

Lady's Steps

1.	Left foot small step to side	cha
2.	Right foot half closes to left foot	cha
3.	Left foot small step to side	Cha

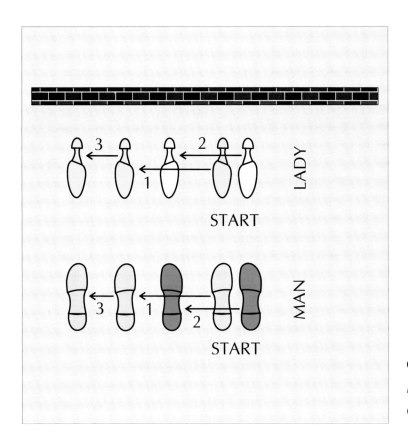

Cha Cha Cha
MAN and LADY
Chasse to left

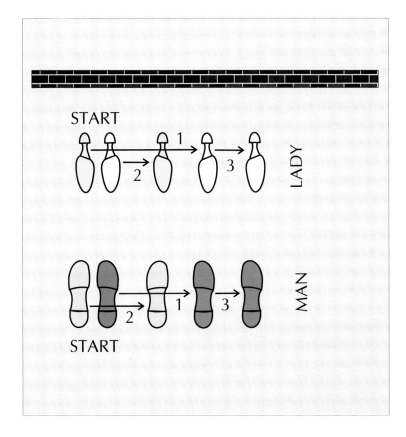

Cha Cha Cha
MAN and LADY
Chasse to right

First Steps - Cha Cha Cha

Cha Cha Cha Basic Movement

This is a dance which does not progress round the room, which means that you may face in any direction at the start of the figure. The man holds the lady about 30 centimetres (a foot) away from himself with his right hand on the lady's back and side just above the waist. He holds the lady's right hand comfortably in his left hand at about chest level and half way between the couple.

If you have a partner you can practise first with your hands on partner's shoulders, if not you can try the figure holding a chair in front of you.

Listen for the 'cha cha cha' triplet in the music and as soon as the last 'cha' has ended follow with the steps:

Man's Steps

1.	Left foot forward - not a long step	Step
2.	Right foot remains in place but weight is taken back on to it	Step
3.	Left foot small step to side	cha
4.	Right foot half closes to left foot	cha
5.	Left foot small step to side	Cha
6.	Right foot back - not a long step	Step
7.	Left foot remains in place but weight is taken forward on to it	Step
8.	Right foot small step forward and to side	cha
9.	Left foot half closes to right foot	cha
10.	Right foot small step to side	Cha

Lady's Steps

1.	Right foot back - not a long step	Step
2.	Left foot remains in place but weight is taken forward on to it	Step
3.	Right foot small step to side	cha
4.	Left foot half closes to right foot	cha
5.	Right foot small step to side	Cha
6.	Left foot forward - not a long step	Step
7.	Right foot remains in place but weight is taken back on to it	Step
8.	Left foot small step back and to side	cha
9.	Right foot half closes to left foot	cha
10.	Left foot small step to side	Cha

No doubt you have noticed that steps 3,4 and 5 are a **cha cha cha chasse** as are steps 8, 9 and 10.

This figure can be repeated. It can be danced without turn but it is much better if a little turn to left is made. For beginners about four full figures to make one complete turn is suitable.

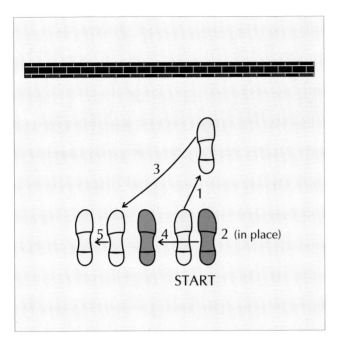

Cha Cha Cha
MAN Basic movement, steps 1-5

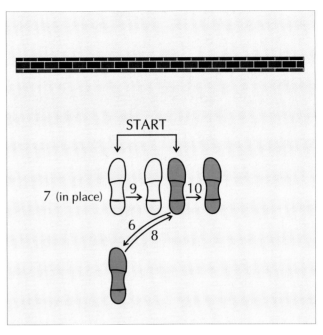

Cha Cha Cha
MAN Basic movement, steps 6-10

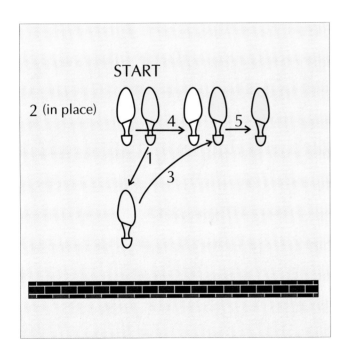

Cha Cha Cha
LADY Basic movement, steps 1-5

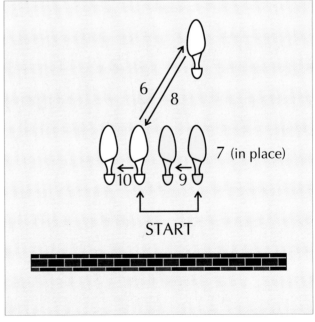

Cha Cha Cha
LADY Basic movement, steps 6-10

Definitions

Definitions

Dancers have a number of special expressions or phrases which they use to describe some aspects of dancing. Now is the time to introduce some of them.

The Holds

The first ones to learn are those which relate to the way you hold your partner. The hold described in the chapter **How to Learn** earlier in the book is the hold used for most popular dances since the 1920's. It is sometimes called the **normal** hold but I will refer to it as the **closed hold** showing that you stand in close proximity to your partner.

In closed hold the bodies of the couple touch - quite firmly. The lady is not absolutely central with respect to her partner. Her right hip will be somewhere in the centre of the man's hips and certainly to the man's right of his left hip.

The other important hold is that used for jive, cha cha cha or rumba and, reflecting the fact that your partner is anything from 30 to 60 centimetres (a foot or two feet) apart from and facing you, is called the **open hold**.

The man holds the lady's right hand in his left a little above waist height. His right hand rests on the lady's left side or waist.

The Directions

Dancers have to understand the direction in which any step is taken relative to the room - it is assumed that the dance is taking place in a room but there are times when it could be outside - and even in a room the shape and size can vary considerably. There are rectangular ballrooms, round ballrooms and even some shaped like a letter 'L'.

For the moment consider only rectangular ballrooms shaped something like this page. You will join the dance by coming on to the dance floor from somewhere near one of the outer walls. Let us suppose that the right hand vertical edge of this page is one wall of our ballroom. You have been sitting or standing near it.

Stand with your back to the wall and you will be looking straight across the room - or if you are relating to this page of the book - to the left hand vertical edge. Enter the floor just a little way, it will depend on the size of the room, but certainly no more than a quarter of the way across the room.

Turn a right angle to your right. In the case of the page of this book you will now be facing the top short edge of the page. The wall on your right side (the long right hand vertical edge of this page) is 'the wall' to which I will be referring if I say 'face the wall'.

If you stand with this wall on your right side we say you are facing **line of dance**. If you walk forward you will soon reach a point near the corner. When you feel you are near enough then you must negotiate the corner with an appropriate figure . Then you are ready to move along the next line of dance which, using our analogy of the page of the book, would be along the top edge.

So in a rectangular room the line of dance goes round a smaller rectangle moving in an anti-clockwise direction.

If you stand facing line of dance and then turn a right angle to your right this will leave you facing the nearest wall and this direction is called **facing wall**. Similarly if you face line of dance and then make a quarter turn to the left I will say you are **facing inwards**.

Start facing wall and then turn a right angle to right and you will have your back to the line of dance - reverting to our analogy, using the page of this book, your back will be towards the top short edge and you will be facing the bottom short edge - this is called **backing line of dance**.

There are two intermediate directions I shall use. If you face line of dance and turn to the right half way towards facing wall, that is half of a right angle, you will be facing slanting towards the wall which is called **diagonally to wall**. Similarly if you face the line of dance and turn half a right angle to left you will be facing slanting in to the room, or what I will call **diagonally inwards**.

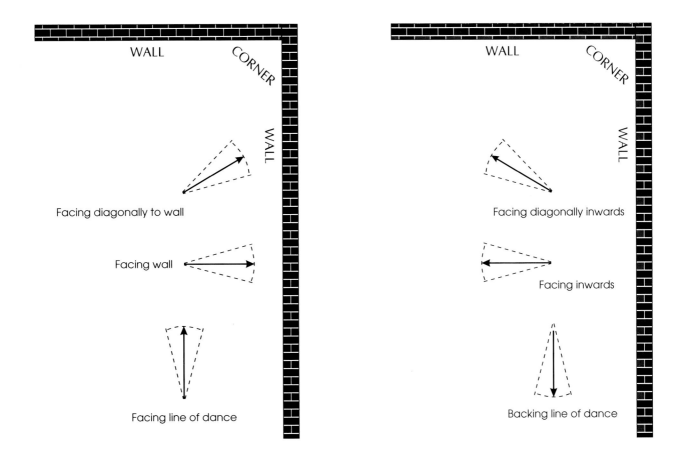

Some important directions

Body Positions

When dancing in closed hold, as in the social foxtrot, waltz and so on, the partners are normally facing each other. The lady is a little to the man's right so that her right foot is not exactly pointing towards the man's left foot but is a few centimetres to the man's right - lady's left - of the position they would be in when precisely opposite each other.

This position is not maintained all the time. Sometimes the man takes a step forward placing his right foot to his left side of the lady's right foot. This sort of step is common in some dances so let us consider it in some detail. If you have a partner to practise with try this out with hands on partner's shoulders, otherwise hold a chair in front of you to get an idea of where your partner is.

Definitions

It is possible to reach this special type of step from a number of different positions. Easiest, however, is to precede the special position with a step to the side on the left foot as man; lady, of course, stepping to side with the right foot. This leaves the couple standing with feet apart - say 30 to 45 centimetres (a foot to one and a half feet) - with man feeling his weight over his left foot and lady with her weight settled on to her right foot.

The next step, as man, is to step forward with the right foot, but in doing so also to cross the right foot slightly across the left foot. If the step is taken in this way it will be found possible to step to the left, as man, of both your partner's feet. When you are experienced it is quite possible to do this without any other change in position, but until that stage is reached you may find it helps to allow the lady's body to move a little to her left, that is man's right, to make sure that there is room for the step.

Steps taken in this way are taken, we say, **outside partner**. In all simple figures there will be a step to the side or forwards or backwards before the step taken outside partner. In the simple figures it is usually the man who is stepping forward in to the position and when he does so the lady is said to have **partner outside**. If the lady steps forward outside partner, as she does sometimes, then the man has **partner outside**.

Open Position

In many figures in dances where open hold is normal - that is the hold where man and lady do not have body contact - a position called **open position** often happens.

When in open position the man is standing just over half a metre (about one and a half to two feet) away from partner and facing her. He holds her only with his left hand, which has hold of the lady's right hand, normally at about waist level. Do not grip the lady's hand too firmly, she will not thank you; similarly the lady's hold of the man's hand must not be too fierce.

Take care in the descriptions which follow not to confuse **open hold** with **open position**. Remember, open hold means the man will be holding his partner with both hands but not in body contact. Open position refers to the relative position of the bodies and the man holds the lady with his left hand only.

Open position

Promenade Position

Another important position is called **promenade position**. When the man steps forward normally the lady will step back - there are times however when the man and lady will both step forward with the couple both facing roughly in the same direction. This comes about by the lady turning her right side away from the man's left side after they have been in closed hold. This leaves the couple still in body contact on the man's right and the lady's left side but a gap between the man's left and lady's right sides.

In this position it is possible for both man and lady to step forward in the same direction. When the man steps forward on his right foot the lady will be stepping forward on her left foot and man and lady will be stepping through a space remaining between their other supporting feet, that is the man's left and lady's right foot.

Definitions

It is the man's job to guide the lady to the figure - to 'lead' her. He does this by pressing on the lady's back in a rather special way with his right hand. The right hand is held on the lady's back and the bottom of the hand will be found near the lady's side. While dancing normally there is just a little pressure from the man's right hand, say enough to hold a sheet of paper against the lady's back and stop it from falling to the floor. To make the lady turn to her right to achieve the promenade position the man increases the pressure from his right hand especially with the bottom (or 'heel') of the hand.

This pressure, which needs to be positive without squeezing all the breath out of the lady, tells the lady (and almost forces her) to make the turn needed. Promenade position should not be achieved by the man pushing forward with his left hand. This is more confusing to the lady and, as a lead, not so readily understood.

We have now reached a stage where you should be able to dance a little to something like three quarters of the music which might be played at any function where there is dancing, other than specialised events such as Scottish dancing, Old Time dancing and so on.

Promenade position

Waltz

Introduction

The waltz is probably the most popular dance of all time. In one form or another it has been a part of the dance scene for longer than any other dance. It is amusing to reflect that it was regarded with unease and met much hostility when it was introduced.

The music is in 3/4 time, that is to say there are three beats in each bar of music and the first beat is played with much more emphasis than the other two. This strong beat coincides with a forward or backward step in all the simple figures. In most of the simple figures one step is taken to each beat of music. Modern waltz music is played at 30 bars a minute. Danced in closed hold, it is led mainly through the body.

Waltz - Closed Change
(Man starting with right foot)

Man's Steps

1.	Right foot forward	One
2.	Left foot to side and slightly forward	Two
3.	Right foot closes to left foot	Three

Lady's Steps

1.	Left foot back	One
2.	Right foot to side and slightly back	Two
3.	Left foot closes to right foot	Three

Waltz- Closed Change
(Man starting with left foot)

Man's Steps

4.	Left foot forward	One
5.	Right foot to side and slightly forward	Two
6.	Left foot closes to right foot	Three

Lady's Steps

4.	Right foot back	One
5.	Left foot to side and slightly back	Two
6.	Right foot closes to left foot	Three

The two closed change steps may be joined together one after the other and repeated as often as required. To do this the man will have to face line of dance. It is possible to move round the room doing only this so long as you curve to the left when approaching a corner so as to move along the next side of the room.

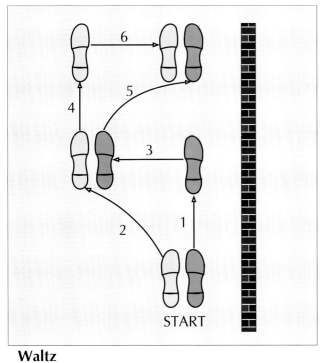

Waltz

MAN Closed changes on right
then left foot

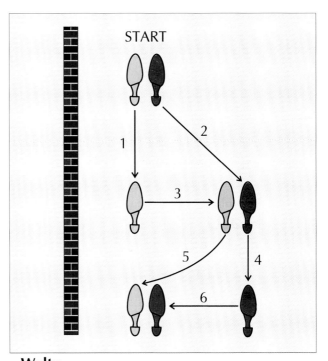

Waltz

LADY Closed changes on lady's left
then with lady's right foot

Step 4
Closed Changes

Waltz

Quarter Turns
(Man starts facing slanting towards the nearest wall, that is, diagonally to wall)

Man's Steps

1.	Right foot forward.	One
2.	Left foot to side, turning to right to face wall.	Two
3.	Right foot closes to left foot, making sure that the weight is taken on to the right foot, still turning to right.	Three
4.	Left foot back.	One
5.	Right foot to side.	Two
6.	Left foot closes to right foot, making sure weight is changed to left foot.	Three
7.	Right foot back.	One
8.	Left foot to side, turning to left to face wall.	Two
9.	Right foot closes to left foot, still turning to left.	Three
10.	Left foot forward.	One
11.	Right foot to side.	Two
12.	Left foot closes to right foot.	Three

Lady's Steps

1.	Left foot back.	One
2.	Right foot to side, turning to right.	Two
3.	Left foot closes to right foot, still turning to right and making sure weight is changed on to left foot.	Three
4.	Right foot forward.	One
5.	Left foot to side.	Two
6.	Right foot closes to left foot making sure weight is changed to right foot.	Three
7.	Left foot forward.	One
8.	Right foot to side, turning to left.	Two
9.	Left foot closes to right foot, still turning to left.	Three
10.	Right foot back.	One
11.	Left foot to side.	Two
12.	Right foot closes to left foot.	Three

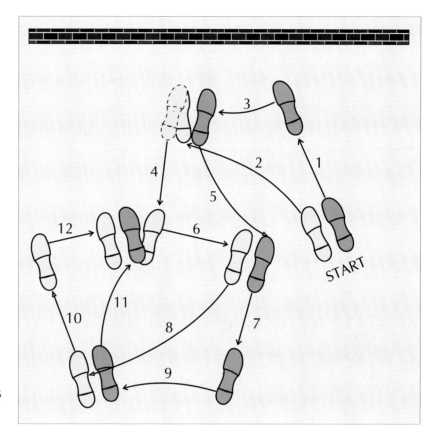

Waltz
MAN Quarter turns

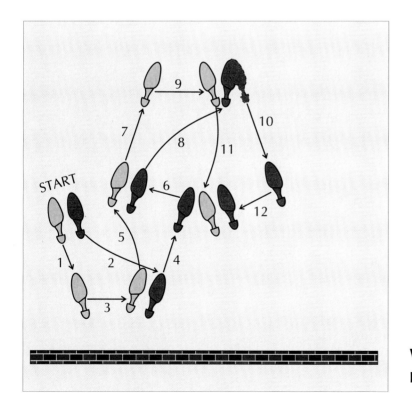

Waltz
LADY Quarter turns

The quarter turn in waltz may be repeated as often as desired, it can then be followed by the right or natural turn, which I shall now describe.

Waltz

Natural Turn
(Man starts facing slanting towards wall, that is, diagonally to wall)

Man's Steps

1.	Right foot forward, turning to right.	*One*
2.	Left foot to side, still turning to right.	*Two*
3.	Right foot closes to left foot - now backing down room with wall on left side.	*Three*
4.	Left foot back, turning to right.	*One*
5.	Right foot to side, still turning to right.	*Two*
6.	Left foot closes to right foot - now facing slanting into room, i.e. diagonally inwards.	*Three*

Lady's Steps

1.	Left foot back, turning to right.	*One*
2.	Right foot to side, still turning to right.	*Two*
3.	Left foot closes to right - now facing down room.	*Three*
4.	Right foot forward, turning to right.	*One*
5.	Left foot to side, still turning to right.	*Two*
6.	Right foot closes to left foot - now backing slanting into room.	*Three*

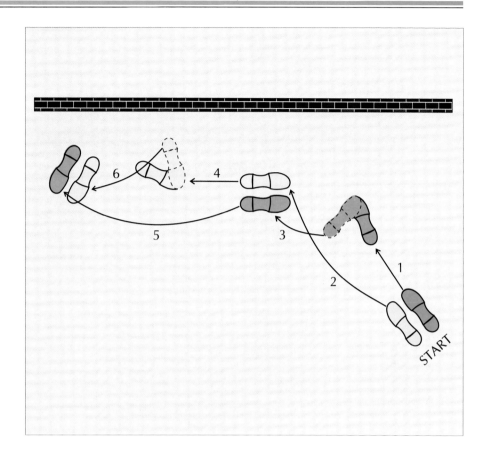

Waltz
MAN Natural (right) turn

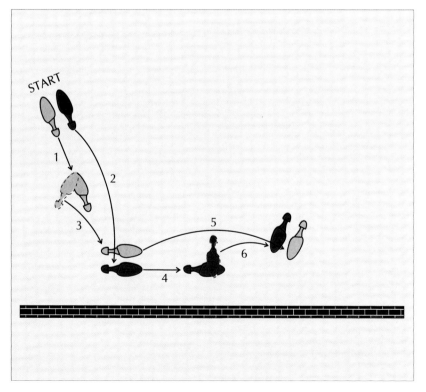

Waltz
LADY Natural (right) turn

The natural turn leaves the man facing diagonally inwards and ready to step off with his right foot. From this position he can dance a closed change step starting with his right foot and then the reverse (or left) turn, the description of which follows:

Waltz

Reverse Turn

Man's Steps

1.	*Left foot forward diagonally inwards, turning to left.*	*One*
2.	*Right foot to side, still turning to left.*	*Two*
3.	*Left foot closes to right foot - now backing line of dance.*	*Three*
4.	*Right foot back, turning body to left.*	*One*
5.	*Left foot to side, still turning to left.*	*Two*
6.	*Right foot closes to left foot - now facing diagonally to wall.*	*Three*

Lady's Steps

1.	*Right foot back diagonally inwards, turning to left.*	*One*
2.	*Left foot to side, still turning to left.*	*Two*
3.	*Right foot closes to left foot - now facing line of dance.*	*Three*
4.	*Left foot forward, turning to left.*	*One*
5.	*Right foot to side, still turning to left.*	*Two*
6.	*Left foot closes to right foot - now backing diagonally to wall.*	*Three*

Waltz

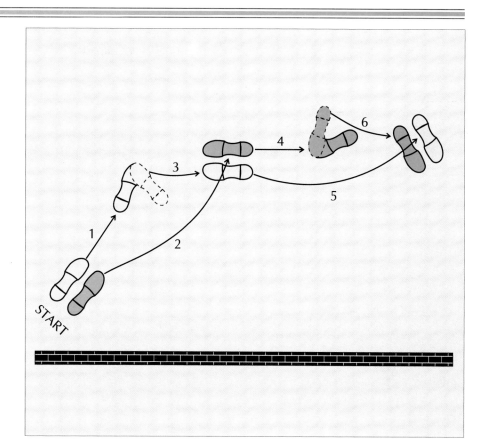

Waltz

MAN Reverse (left) turn

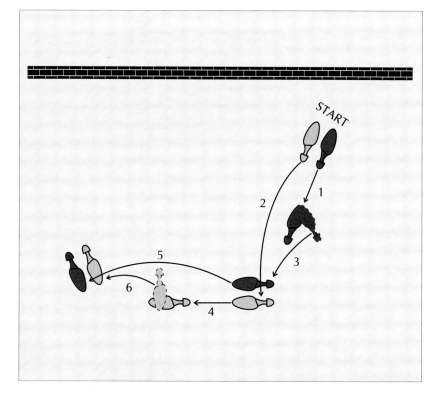

Waltz

LADY Reverse (left) turn

After the reverse turn the man is ready to step towards the wall and use his left foot. He can dance the closed change step starting on the left foot and then go into the natural turn, or he can take the whisk immediately after the reverse turn. The whisk and chasse will be described next. This group is extremely popular and is danced by all experienced dancers.

33

Waltz

Whisk and Chasse

Man's Steps

1.	Left foot forward diagonally to wall.	One
2.	Right foot to side and slightly forward.	Two
3.	Left foot crosses behind right foot in promenade position.	Three
4.	Right foot forward in promenade position along the line of dance.	One
5.	Left foot to side and slightly forward along the line of dance.	Two
6.	Right foot closes to left foot.	and
7.	Left foot to side and slightly forward.	Three

Lady's Steps

1.	Right foot back diagonally to wall.	One
2.	Left foot side and back, starting to turn to right to promenade position.	Two
3.	Right foot crosses behind left foot in promenade position, now facing diagonally inwards.	Three
4.	Left foot forward in promenade position along line of dance.	One
5.	Right foot to side, turning to left.	Two
6.	Left foot closes to right foot, now backing diagonally to wall, and facing partner.	and
7.	Right foot to side and slightly back.	Three

After the whisk and chasse the man can go into the natural turn. However, the first step of the natural turn, when taken after the chasse, is taken outside partner, that is, taken with the man stepping to his left of both his partner's feet.

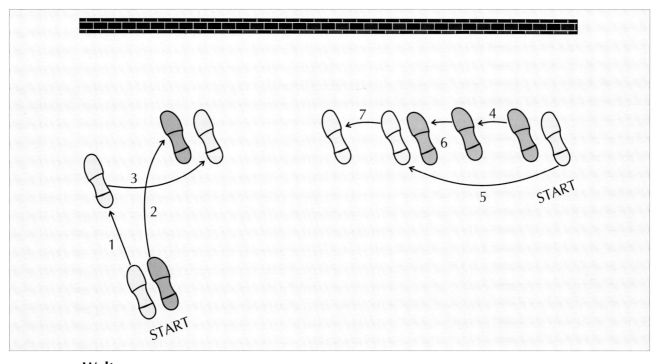

Waltz

MAN Whisk steps 1-3   Chasse from whisk position steps 4-7

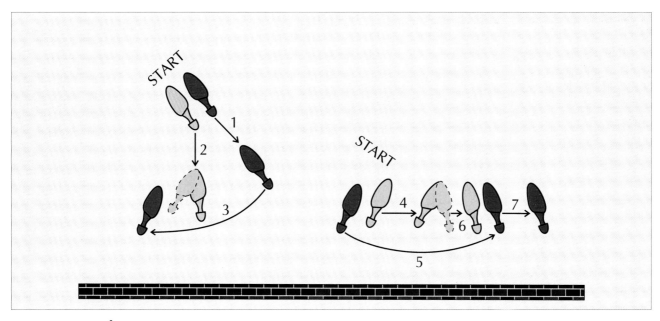

Waltz

LADY Whisk steps 1-3   Chasse from whisk position steps 4-7

Instead of the natural turn the man can dance the natural spin turn, a more advanced figure and perhaps the most popular single figure in all dancing.

Waltz

Natural Spin Turn

This is a figure which is used extensively by all dancers and once you have mastered it you will begin to get a 'feeling' for the movement of dance. Briefly, the couple are moving round the room, and then the man and his partner make a condensed turn, twirling round together. You have seen it, for certain.

The way to learn this figure, which calls for a little panache, is first to make quite sure that you have learnt the foot patterns and can do them without having to think too much. At this stage we find a figure where the steps for the lady are not the expected opposite of the man's. You will by now expect the lady to step back when the man steps forward and vice versa. Here at one stage the man steps forward and the lady to the side.

Try first the pattern without turn. The first three steps of the natural spin turn are those of the natural turn (page 30/31), so for the moment let us assume that you have done them and you are standing with your back to the line of dance as man, you should be standing with feet together but with the weight firmly over the right foot. There is a pattern of three steps to learn and for these we are going to print the man's and lady's steps side by side so that you can see how they relate to each other.

Man's Steps	Lady's Steps	
1. *Left foot back.*	1. *Right foot forward.*	*One*
2. *Right foot pushes forward a few centimetres and weight is taken forward on it so that you are now standing on right foot only.*	2. *Left foot to side of right foot - feet about 30 centimetres (a foot) apart. This will bring the man's right foot more or less between the lady's feet.*	*Two*
3. *Left foot placed to side of right foot - feet about 30 centimetres (a foot) apart*	3. *Right foot moves sideways and finishes to lady's left of man's left foot*	*Three*

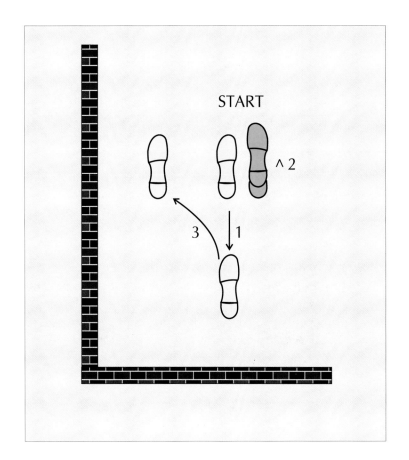

Waltz

MAN Exercise for spin turn (steps 4-6 of spin turn without making turn)

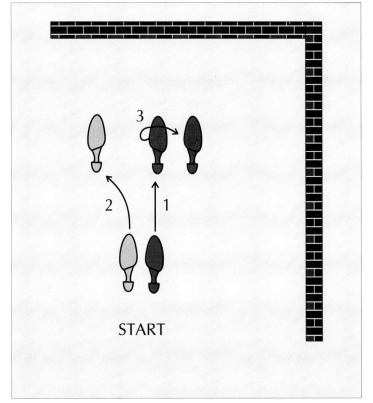

Waltz

LADY Exercise for spin turn (steps 4-6 of spin turn without making turn)

Waltz

First make sure that you have the pattern clear in your mind. For the man it is back, forward, side. For the lady it is forward, side, side.

Now try the same pattern but turn just a little to right on the three steps. Repeat this with a little turn until it presents no difficulty. Now do it again but increase the amount of turn you make. The man starts these three steps backing line of dance and by now he should be able to face inwards across the room by the end of the third step, thus having made a 90 degree turn. Keep practising until you can turn at least twice as much, that is to say until you can turn to face down the line of dance at the end of the three steps.

The lady too must gradually increase her turn, first making sure that she can turn to face outwards towards the nearest wall having started facing down line of dance and gradually increasing the amount of turn until she can finish the three steps with her back to the line of dance.

The amount of turn indicated so far is a half turn and this is the smallest amount of turn which can reasonably be made on the three steps of the actual 'spin'. Experienced dancers will make about three quarters of a full turn. To achieve even half a turn needs a quite deliberate and conscious effort to turn strongly - indeed, as the name of the figure says - to spin.

The man must hold the lady very firmly at this stage and make the positive effort to spin round taking his partner with him. It is not difficult, but it does need some confidence.

There are nine steps in the full spin turn in the waltz. The pattern you have been practising is the middle group of three, that is steps 4,5 and 6. All nine steps will now be described.

Third Step of Whisk

When taken after Spin turn

First Step Reverse Turn

Taken after Spin turn

Spin Turn

Man's Steps

(Man starts facing diagonally to wall)

(For steps 1-5 see diagram on page 31)

1.	Right foot forward.	One
2.	Left foot to side turning to right.	Two
3.	Right foot closes to left foot, taking weight on to right foot when it reaches position, still turning so that man is backing line of dance.	Three
4.	Left foot back a short step, turning strongly to right and keeping right foot held forward as turn is made.	One
5.	Right foot moves forward a few centimetres - placing it between lady's feet	Two
6.	Left foot a short step to side, still turning so that man is facing diagonally to wall.	Three
7.	Right foot back.	One
8.	Left foot to side, turning to left.	Two
9.	Right foot closes to left foot, still turning, to leave man facing diagonally inwards.	Three

This figure can now be followed by the reverse turn.

TIP

It is possible for the man to turn more to the right on the first six steps. This will leave the man facing diagonally to wall at the end of the figure and, instead of then dancing the reverse turn, he will dance either a closed change step on left foot or a whisk.

Waltz

MAN Steps 4-9 of spin turn (taken after steps 1-3 of natural turn)

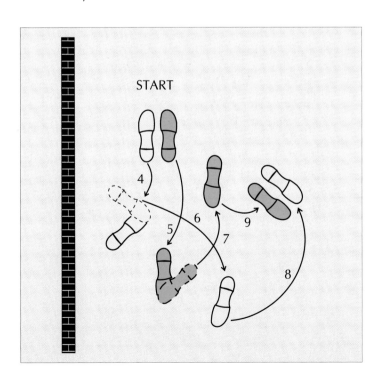

Waltz

Lady's Steps

(For steps 1-3 see diagram on page 31)

1.	*Left foot back.*	*One*
2.	*Right foot to side, turning to right.*	*Two*
3.	*Left foot closes to right foot, taking weight on to left foot when it reaches position, still turning to right.*	*Three*
4.	*Right foot forward a short step, turning strongly to right.*	*One*
5.	*Left foot a short step to side, still turning strongly to right. At this point the lady steps to side and man is placing his foot forward between both the lady's feet.*	*Two*
6.	*Right foot is moved a few centimetres to side, having first continued strong turn on left foot. In moving the right foot to position good dancers brush the right foot against the left foot before moving it the few centimetres to side.*	*Three*
7.	*Left foot forward.*	*One*
8.	*Right foot to side, turning to left.*	*Two*
9.	*Left foot closes to right foot, taking weight on to left foot when it reaches position.*	*Three*

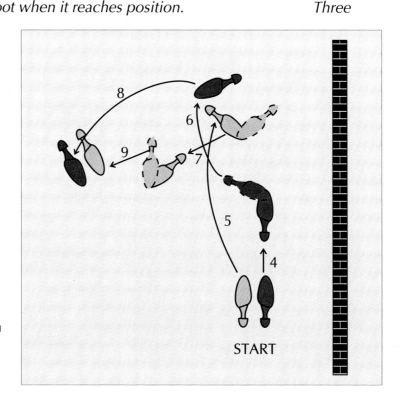

Waltz

LADY Steps 4-9 of spin turn (taken after steps 1-3 of natural turn)

Samba

Introduction

Samba music originated in Brazil. It has a tradition reaching back hundreds of years and has been associated with some voodoo religions such as Macumba. In this century first the maxixe and more recently the samba as we know it have been popular dances. It is a fairly easy dance, redolent of the carnival atmosphere with which dancing is so often associated in Brazil.

The music can be assumed to be in 4/4 time though it is often written in 2/4 time. The steps should be learned in open hold and are mostly danced this way. In crowded conditions it is possible to dance in closed hold, but without the firm body contact characteristic of waltz.

The rhythm is fairly brisk and each bar of music has three steps fitted to the bar in the figures described, though there are other rhythms used by more advanced dancers. The count for each group of three steps is 'one, a, Two'. The 'one' and the 'a' are both fitted in to the first half of the bar while the 'Two' fills the second half of the bar and takes the same time as the 'one' and the 'a' added together.

The count 'one' lasts longer than the count 'a' and since a reasonably long step is normally put to the count 'one' there is often a feeling of coming to rest on the third count 'Two'.

On all the figures in the samba described here - but not on all the figures in the dance itself - there is a softening or slight bending of the knees on the step counted 'one', this is followed by a straightening of the knee on the count of 'a'. The knee is bent slightly as the weight change is made on the count 'Two', then straightened again, still on count 'Two'.

Do not overdo this action, just a little will give you the characteristic bounce action of the samba.

Samba

Step 4 Natural Basic Movement

Samba

Natural Basic Movement
(Start in closed hold. May be danced with or without turn to right)

Man's Steps

1.	Right foot forward	*one*
2.	Left foot closes to right foot	*'a'*
3.	Right foot remains in place and weight is transferred to it	*Two*
4.	Left foot back	*one*
5.	Right foot closes to left foot	*'a'*
6.	Left foot remains in place and weight is transferred to it	*Two*

Lady's Steps

1.	Left foot back	*one*
2.	Right foot closes to left foot	*'a'*
3.	Left foot remains in place and weight is transferred to it	*Two*
4.	Right foot forward	*one*
5.	Left foot closes to right foot	*'a'*
6.	Right foot remains in place and weight is transferred to it	*Two*

The figure may be repeated as often as you wish. The figure is described without turn but it is possible to turn a little to the right throughout - one full turn to the right can be made spread over four natural basics.

Soon you will want to change to another figure and this is done most easily by dancing the first half of the figure described above and then following with the reverse basic. A description of this follows.

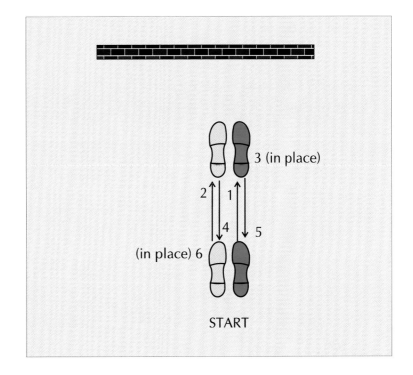

Samba
MAN Natural basic

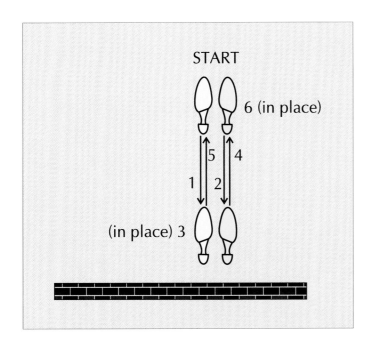

Samba
LADY Natural basic

Samba

The Samba bounce action seen from side

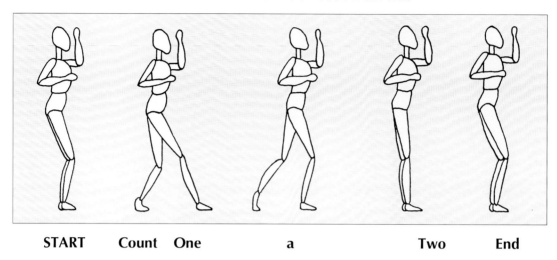

| START | Count One | a | Two | End |

Reverse Basic Movement

(Start in closed hold. May be danced with or without turn to left)

Man's Steps

1.	Left foot forward	one
2.	Right foot closes to left foot	'a'
3.	Left foot remains in place and weight is transferred to it	Two
4.	Right foot back	one
5.	Left foot closes to right foot	'a'
6.	Right foot remains in place and weight is transferred to it	Two

Lady's Steps

1.	Right foot back	one
2.	Left foot closes to right foot	'a'
3.	Right foot remains in place and weight is transferred to it	Two
4.	Left foot forward	one
5.	Right foot closes to left foot	'a'
6.	Left foot remains in place and weight is transferred to it	Two

The reverse basic can be repeated as desired. It is described without turn but turn can be made to the left. One full turn to the left can be made over four full reverse basic figures.

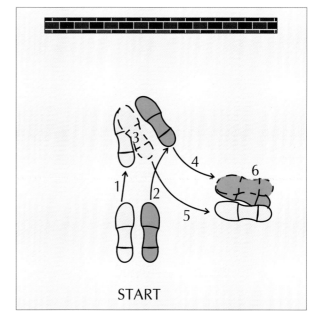

Samba

MAN Reverse basic movement
(with turn)

START

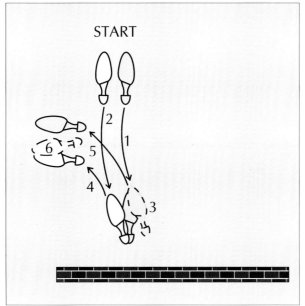

START

Samba

LADY Reverse basic movement
(with turn)

The change back to the natural basic figure can be made after the first half of the reverse basic.

The following amalgamation of the two figures should be practised: the man should start facing wall, dance four full natural basic movements turning to right so that at the end of the fourth natural basic he is facing wall again; dance the forward half of the natural basic, then step forward with left foot into reverse basic movement and dance four full reverse basic movements turning to the left until man is facing wall again; now dance the forward half of the reverse basic movement.

This complete amalgamation can be repeated as often as you like.

Both the natural and reverse basics, and all other simple figures, can be danced in closed or open hold.

Samba

Progressive Basic Movement

(Start facing diagonally to wall)

Man's Steps

1.	Right foot forward	*one*
2.	Left foot closes to right foot	*'a'*
3.	Right foot remains in place and weight is transferred to it	*Two*
4.	Left foot to side	*one*
5.	Right foot closes to left foot	*'a'*
6.	Left foot remains in place and weight is transferred to it	*Two*

Lady's Steps

1.	Left foot back	*one*
2.	Right foot closes to left foot	*'a'*
3.	Left foot remains in place and weight is transferred to it	*Two*
4.	Right foot to side	*one*
5.	Left foot closes to right foot	*'a'*
6.	Right foot remains in place and weight is transferred to it	*Two*

The progressive basic movement can follow the natural basic movement when it finishes facing diagonally to wall.

After the progressive basic movement the outside movement described next can be taken.

Samba

Samba
MAN Progressive basic

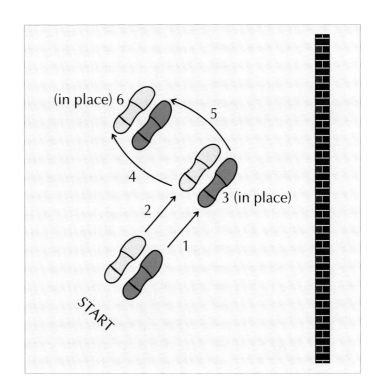

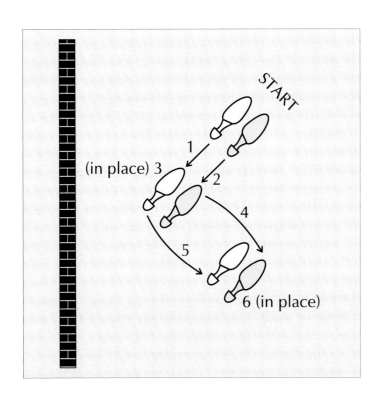

Samba
LADY Progressive basic

Samba

Outside Movement

Man's Steps

1.	Right foot forward	one
2.	Left foot closes to right foot, turning to left	''a'
3.	Right foot remains in place and weight is transferred to it, still turning to left.	Two
4.	Left foot back, lady stepping forward with her right foot to man's right side (ie partner outside).	one
5.	Right foot closes to left foot.	'a'
6.	Left foot remains in place and weight is transferred to it.	Two
7.	Right foot forward to man's left of both lady's feet (ie outside partner)	one
8.	Left foot closes to right foot, turning to right	'a'
9.	Right foot remains in place and weight is transferred to it, man should now be facing partner.	Two
10.	Left foot back	one
11.	Right foot closes to left foot	'a'
12.	Left foot remains in place and weight is transferred to it.	Two

Lady's Steps

1.	Left foot back.	one
2.	Right foot closes to left foot, turning to left.	'a'
3.	Left foot remains in place and weight is transferred to it, still turning to left.	Two
4.	Right foot forward to lady's left side of both partner's feet (ie outside partner).	one
5.	Left foot closes to right foot.	'a'
6.	Right foot remains in place and weight is transferred to it.	Two
7.	Left foot back, partner stepping to lady's right side of both feet (ie partner outside).	one
8.	Right foot closes to left foot, turning to right.	'a'
9.	Left foot remains in place and weight is transferred to it, lady now faces partner.	Two
10.	Right foot forward.	one
11.	Left foot closes to right foot.	'a'
12.	Right foot remains in place and weight is transferred to it.	Two

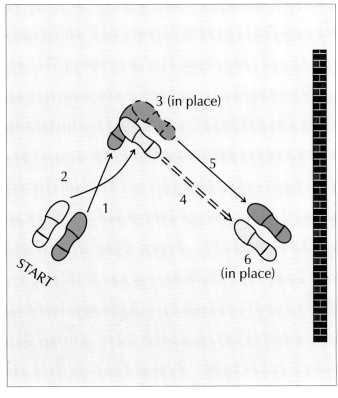

Step 4 Outside Movement

Samba

MAN Outside movement steps 1-6
(the dotted line on step 4
indicates that this step is
taken with partner outside)

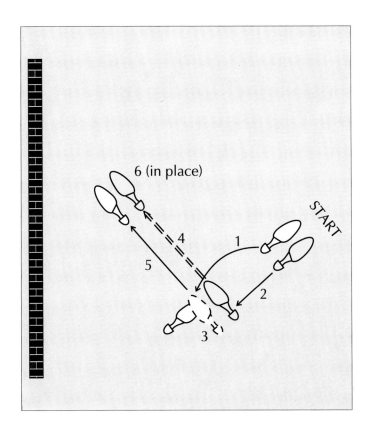

Samba

LADY Outside movement, steps 1-6
(the dotted line on step 4
indicates that this step is
taken outside partner)

Quickstep

Introduction

For many years this was the most popular dance in the ballrooms and was regarded as the easiest by many dancers. It is danced to 4/4 music played fairly quickly. The rhythm is the same as that used for social foxtrot but is quicker.

Advanced dancers use many intricate patterns in this dance but the fundamental pleasure to be gained from the dance is created by the flow round the room.

This is another dance which uses a form of the quarter turns. This is the best figure with which to start your study.

Quarter Turns
(Man starts facing diagonally to wall)

This is the first figure in the quickstep and can be repeated in the same way - with one small difference - as the quarter turns in the social foxtrot and the waltz.

The difference arises from the fact that the figure can start either in line with partner (that is with man's right foot following the lady's left foot on the first step) or outside partner (here the man's right foot does not follow the line of the lady's left foot but is placed forward to the man's left side of the lady's right foot). The description to follow will help make this clear.

Man's Steps

1.	*Right foot forward.*	*Slow*
2.	*Left foot to side, turning to right to face wall.*	*Quick*
3.	*Right foot closes to left foot, taking weight fully on to right foot, still turning to right.*	*Quick*
4.	*Left foot to side a small step.*	*Slow*
5.	*Right foot back.*	*Slow*
6.	*Left foot to side, turning to left to face wall.*	*Quick*
7.	*Right foot closes to left foot, taking weight fully on to right foot, still turning to left.*	*Quick*
8.	*Left foot to side a small step.*	*Slow*

Lady's Steps

1.	*Left foot back.*	*Slow*
2.	*Right foot to side, turning to right.*	*Quick*
3.	*Left foot closes to right foot, taking weight fully on to left foot, still turning to right.*	*Quick*
4.	*Right foot to side a small step.*	*Slow*
5.	*Left foot forward.*	*Slow*
6.	*Right foot to side, turning to left.*	*Quick*
7.	*Left foot closes to right foot, taking weight fully on to left foot, still turning to left.*	*Quick*
8.	*Right foot to side a small step.*	*Slow*

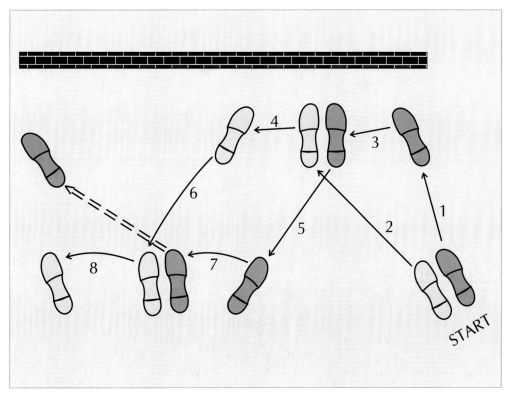

Step 8 ends the man's steps and he has his feet apart. To repeat the figure the first step - right foot forward - is taken by crossing the right foot slightly across the left foot and leg. This will allow the first step of the repeated quarter turn to be taken 'outside partner'.

Quickstep

MAN

Quarter turns including step outside partner to follow (un-numbered)

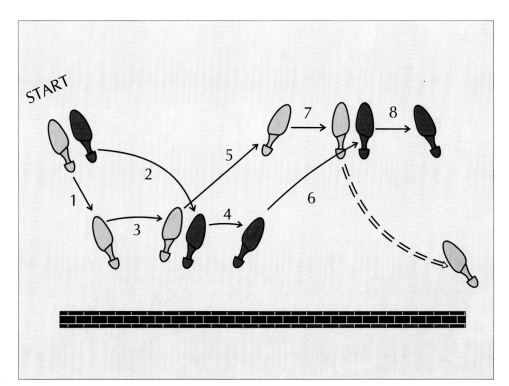

Quickstep

LADY

Quarter turns including step with partner outside to follow (un-numbered)

Quickstep

Lock Step

(This figure is normally started by stepping outside partner and moves diagonally to wall. It follows the quarter turns very well)

Man's Steps

1.	Right foot forward, stepping to left of both partner's feet, (ie outside partner).	*Slow*
2.	Left foot forward, turning body slightly to right.	*Quick*
3.	Right foot crosses behind left foot - feet should not be too close together but about 15 centimetres (six inches) apart.	*Quick*
4.	Left foot forward and a little to side, a small step. The sideways movement of the foot is to allow space to take the next step forward outside partner.	*Slow*

Lady's Steps

1.	Left foot back, partner is stepping outside on this step.	*Slow*
2.	Right foot back, turning body slightly to right.	*Quick*
3.	Left foot crosses in front of right foot - feet should not be too close together but about 15 centimetres (six inches) apart.	*Quick*
4.	Right foot a short step back.	*Slow*

The lock step can be followed by any figure started by man stepping forward on right foot outside partner and facing diagonally to wall. So after the lock step the man can dance quarter turns or the natural turn or the spin turn. When you have learnt the quarter turns and lock step this is a good group to practise until you can dance it fairly fluently.

Quickstep

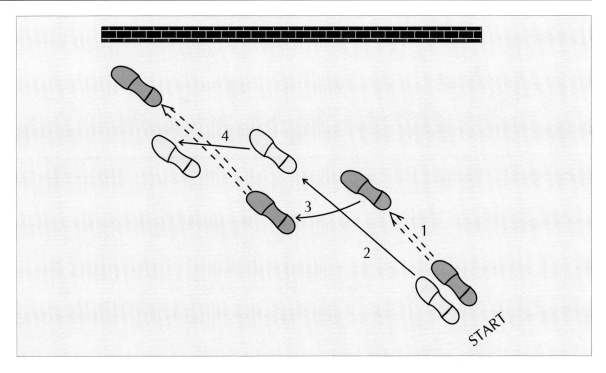

Quickstep

MAN Lock step including step
outside partner to follow
(un-numbered)

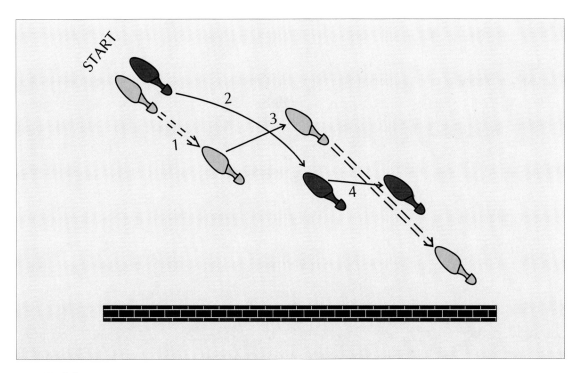

Quickstep

LADY Lock steps including step with partner
outside to follow (un-numbered)

Quickstep

Natural Turn

(This figure is described approaching the corner of the room and when completed moves off along the next wall)

Man's Steps

1.	Right foot forward, diagonally to wall, turning body to right.	Slow
2.	Left foot to side, still turning to right.	Quick
3.	Close right foot to left foot, still turning to right now backing line of dance.	Quick
4.	Left foot back, turning body to right.	Slow
5.	Right foot to side of left foot, small step, having turned to right on left foot - end facing diagonally to next wall.	Slow
6.	Left foot forward, diagonally to wall of new line of dance.	Slow

Note: If this figure is preceded by the progressive chasse or the forward lock step, the first step will be taken outside partner.

Lady's Steps

1.	Left foot back, diagonally to wall, turning body to right.	Slow
2.	Right foot to side, still turning to right.	Quick
3.	Close left foot to right foot - now facing line of dance.	Quick
4.	Right foot forward, turning body to right.	Slow
5.	Left foot to side, still turning to right.	Slow
6.	Brush right foot to left foot and then step back right foot - now backing diagonally to wall of new line of dance.	Slow

Natural Hesitation Turn

This figure can be used either at a corner or along the side of the room. It is very similar to the natural turn just described.

By taking a wider step on step 5 and allowing an extra "slow' count to allow left foot to close to right foot without changing weight prior to stepping forward (as man) on step 6, you will accomplish the natural turn with hesitation. A chasse reverse turn, described next, is used along the side of the room.

Quickstep

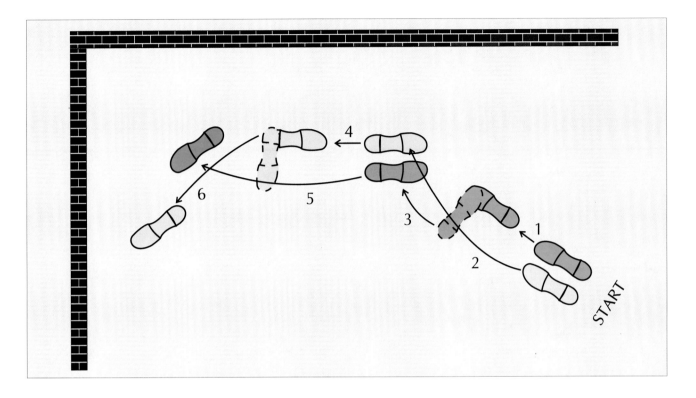

Quickstep
MAN Natural (right) turn

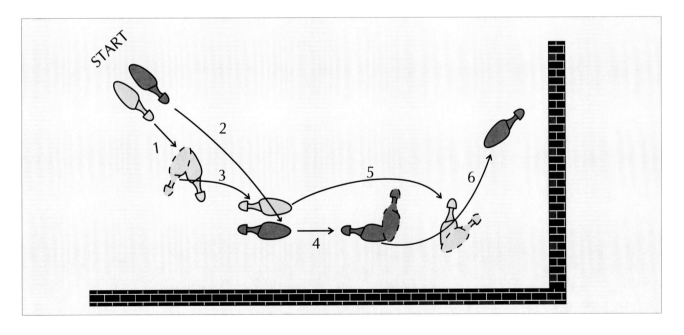

Quickstep
LADY Natural (right) turn

Quickstep

Chasse Reverse Turn
(With progressive chasse ending)

Man's Steps

1.	Left foot forward facing diagonally inwards, turning body to left.	*Slow*
2.	Right foot to side, still turning to left.	*Quick*
3.	Left foot closes to right foot, turning to left - now backing line of dance.	*Quick*
4.	Right foot back, turning body to left.	*Slow*
5.	Left foot to side, still turning body to left.	*Quick*
6.	Right foot closes to left foot - now facing diagonally to wall.	*Quick*
7.	Left foot to side and slightly forward.	*Slow*

Lady's Steps

1.	Right foot back diagonally inwards, turning body to left.	*Slow*
2.	Left foot to side, still turning to left.	*Quick*
3.	Right foot closes to right foot - now facing line of dance.	*Quick*
4.	Left foot forward, turning body to left.	*Slow*
5.	Right foot to side, still turning body to left.	*Quick*
6.	Left foot closes to right foot - now backing diagonally to wall.	*Quick*
7.	Right foot to side and slightly back.	*Slow*

After the chasse reverse turn the man is facing diagonally to wall and is in a position to dance any of the figures which start in that direction on the right foot and stepping outside partner. These are the quarter turns, the lock step, the natural turn and the natural hesitation turn.

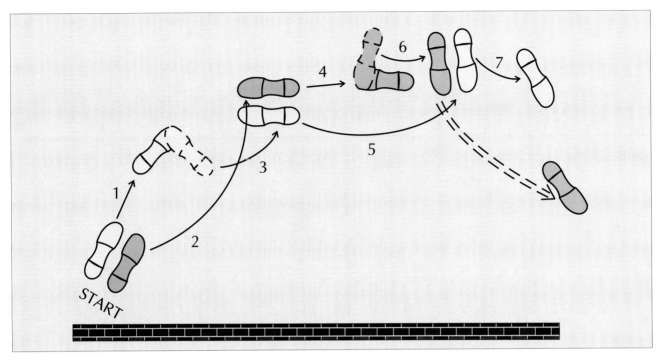

Quickstep

MAN Chasse reverse (left) turn
including step outside partner
to follow (un-numbered)

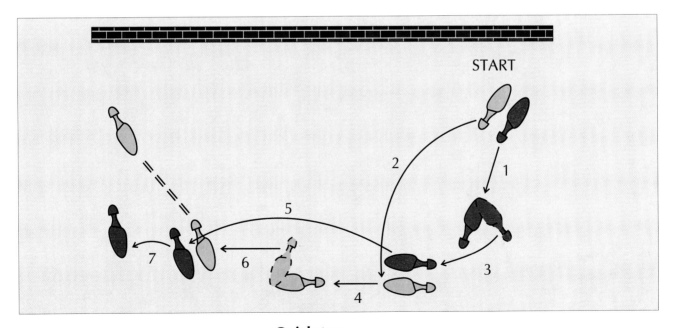

Quickstep

LADY Chasse reverse turn,
including step with partner
outside to follow (un-numbered)

Jive

Introduction

This dance is one which spans the age gap perhaps better than any other. The music is written in 4/4 time - four beats in each bar. This is the same musical time as social foxtrot but the difference is that music suitable for jive has its four beats more heavily accented and the accents are more pronounced on the second and fourth beats than the first and third.

There are generally either three steps or two taken to two beats of music. The count used will be either 'quick, a, Quick' where there are three steps or 'Quick, Quick' where there are two steps.

The counts of 'quick, a' are taken in the same amount of music as the count 'Quick' with the 'quick' - taking longer than the count of 'a'.

Learn first the figure called basic in place, which is an excellent exercise to develop the rhythmic sense.

Basic in Place
(Start in open hold)

Man's Steps

1.	*Left foot in place, take weight fully on to foot.*	Quick
2.	*Right foot in place, take weight fully on to foot.*	Quick
3.	*Left foot a small step to side.*	quick
4.	*Right foot half closed to left foot.*	'a'
5.	*Left foot a small step to side.*	Quick
6.	*Right foot a small step to side.*	quick
7.	*Left foot half closed to right foot.*	'a'
8.	*Right foot to side.*	Quick

Lady's Steps

1.	*Right foot in place, take weight fully on to foot.*	Quick
2.	*Left foot in place, take weight fully on to foot.*	Quick
3.	*Right foot a small step to side.*	quick
4.	*Left foot half closed to right foot.*	'a'
5.	*Right foot a small step to side.*	Quick
6.	*Left foot a small step to side.*	quick
7.	*Right foot half closed to left foot.*	'a'
8.	*Left foot to side.*	Quick

This figure can be repeated. It should be practised until it can be danced fluently. The basic in place can be followed by the basic in fall-away, now described.

Basic in Fall-away

(Man faces lady in open hold and then turns towards his left and, by pushing his left hand forward slightly, guides his partner to turn to her right. This leaves man and partner turned at an angle to each other)

Man's Steps

1.	Left foot back, crossing loosely behind right foot as body turns left.	Quick
2.	Right foot remains in place and weight is taken forward on to it.	Quick
3.	Left foot a small step to side, turning to face partner.	quick
4.	Right foot half closed to left foot.	'a'
5.	Left foot a small step to side.	Quick
6.	Right foot a small step to side.	quick
7.	Left foot half closes to right foot.	'a'
8.	Right foot a small step to side.	Quick

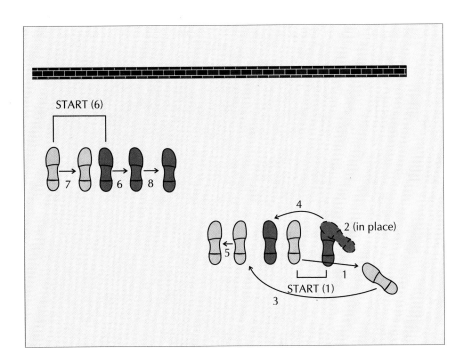

Jive

MAN Basic in fallaway.
The basic steps shown on the right are steps 1-5 inclusive and those on the left are steps 6-8 inclusive. The two halves of the figure are shown separately to avoid superimposition of foot patterns

Jive

Lady's Steps

1. Right foot back, crossing loosely behind left foot as body turns right. — *Quick*

2. Left foot remains in place and weight is taken forward on to it. — *Quick*

3. Right foot a small step to side, turning to face partner. — *quick*

4. Left foot half closed to right foot. — *'a'*

5. Right foot a small step to side. — *Quick*

6. Left foot a small step to side. — *quick*

7. Right foot half closes to left foot. — *'a'*

8. Left foot a small step to side. — *Quick*

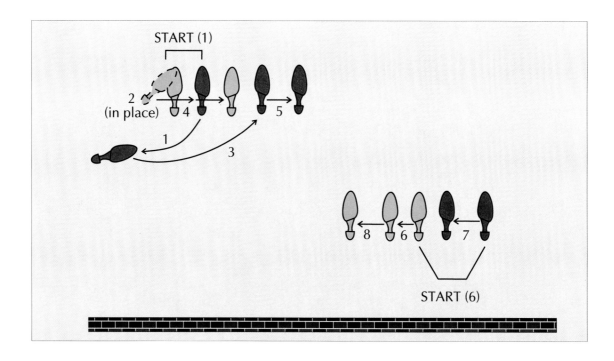

Jive

LADY Basic in fall-away. The basic steps shown on the left are steps 1-5 inclusive and those on the right are steps 6-8 inclusive. The two halves of the figure are shown separately to avoid superimposition of foot patterns

Link
(Start in open hold or open position)

Man's Steps

1.	Left foot back	*Quick*
2.	Right foot remains in place but weight is taken on to it	*Quick*
3.	Left foot a small step forward	*quick*
4.	Right foot closed half way to left foot	*'a'*
5.	Left foot remains in place but weight is taken on to it	*Quick*
6.	Right foot a small step to side	*quick*
7.	Left foot half closes to right foot	*'a'*
8.	Right foot a small step to side	*Quick*

Lady's Steps

1.	Right foot back	*Quick*
2.	Left foot remains in place but weight taken on to it	*Quick*
3.	Right foot a small step forward	*quick*
4.	Left foot closed half way to right foot	*'a'*
5.	Right foot remains in place but weight is taken on to it	*Quick*
6.	Left foot a small step to side	*quick*
7.	Right foot half closes to left foot	*'a'*
8.	Left foot a small step to side	*Quick*

As the man steps back on the first step the lady also steps back. The man leads the lady to this back step by pushing the lady lightly away from him as he starts his step. In order to push the lady he moves his right hand so that it is more on the lady's side than normal. His right hand will leave the lady's side as she moves away from him but he retains his hold of the lady's hand in his left. The man regains his normal open hold as he takes weight forward on to the left foot at the end of the group.

Jive

Change of Place Right to Left
(Start in open hold)

Man's Steps

1.	*Left foot back crossing loosely behind right foot, turn left.*	*Quick*
2.	*Right foot remains in place and weight is taken forward on to it.*	*Quick*
3.	*Left foot a small step to side.*	*quick*
4.	*Right foot half closed to left foot.*	*'a'*
5.	*Left foot a small step to side, lifting left hand to a height a few centimetres above lady's head and removing right hand from lady's back.*	*Quick*
6.	*Right foot forward, turning body slightly left and allowing lady to turn to her right under arch formed by raised hands. Do not grip the lady's right hand in your left - you could stop her from turning altogether.*	*quick*
7.	*Left foot half closes to right foot.*	*'a'*
8.	*Right foot a small step forward, lowering left hand to waist level held in front of body.*	*Quick*

Lady's Steps

1.	*Right foot back crossing loosely behind left foot.*	*Quick*
2.	*Left foot remains in place and weight is taken forward on to it and at the same time turn to left in to man slightly.*	*Quick*
3.	*Right foot a small step to side, still turning body slightly to left.*	*quick*
4.	*Left foot half closed to right foot.*	*'a'*
5.	*Right foot a small step forward, turning strongly to right, turning back to man under raised right hand (and man's left hand).*	*Quick*
6.	*Left foot between side and back, still turning to right.*	*quick*
7.	*Right foot half closes to left foot, still turning to right.*	*'a'*
8.	*Left foot a small step back, now facing partner and holding his left hand in your right.*	*Quick*

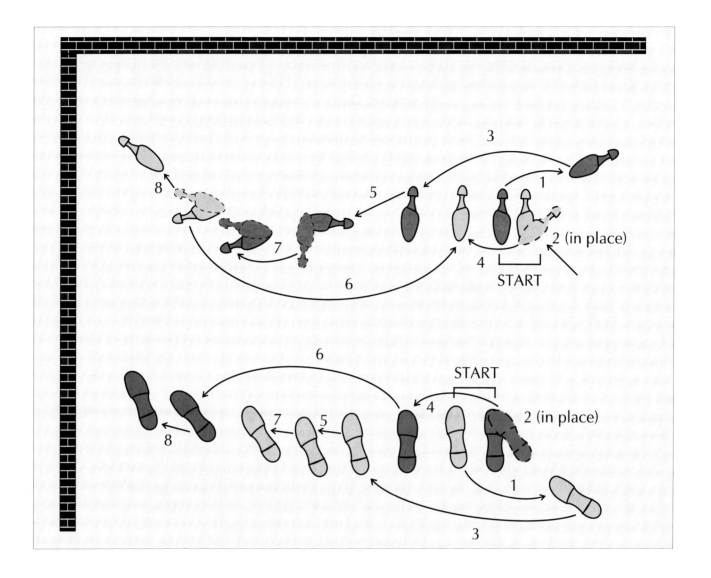

Jive

MAN AND LADY Change of place
right to left

This figure leaves the man holding the lady's right hand in his left - facing the lady and a short distance away from her. Dance now either the change of place left to right, described next, or the link. The link was described with man holding partner in normal position but it can be taken from open hold which is reached at the end of the change of place right to left.

Jive

Change of Place Left to Right

(Start in open position, that is as if you had just danced the change of place right to left)

Man's Steps

1.	Left foot back.	*Quick*
2.	Right foot remains in place and weight is taken forward on to it.	*Quick*
3.	Left foot a small step forward, starting to raise left hand up across body to guide lady to a turn to her left underneath the arch formed by her right and man's left hand - man starts to turn to his right.	*quick*
4.	Right foot half closed to left foot, man's hand now above lady's head height - man continues turn to right.	*'a'*
5.	Left foot a small step back and side, man still turning on both feet, to leave him facing partner.	*Quick*
6.	Right foot a small step forward, starting to lower left arm.	*quick*
7.	Left foot half closed to right foot, lady now having completed turn, man's left hand back to normal height for jive.	*'a'*
8.	Right foot a small step forward.	*Quick*

Lady's Steps

1.	Right foot back.	*Quick*
2.	Left foot remains in place and weight taken forward on to it.	*Quick*
3.	Right foot small step forward, man is raising lady's right hand so she is aware that she needs to turn underneath the arch formed by the lady's right and man's left hand.	*quick*
4.	Left foot half closed to right foot, lady starting to turn to left.	*'a'*
5.	Right foot a small step back, turning strongly to left.	*Quick*
6.	Left foot forward, now facing partner.	*quick*
7.	Right foot half closed to left foot.	*'a'*
8.	Left foot a small step back	*Quick*

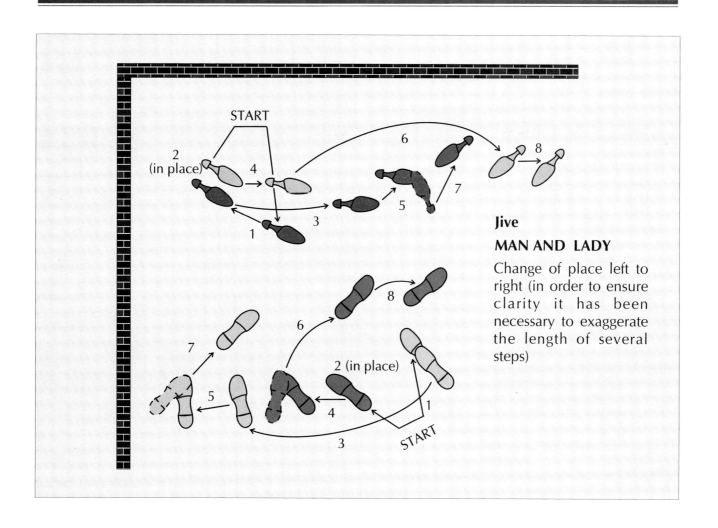

Jive

MAN AND LADY

Change of place left to right (in order to ensure clarity it has been necessary to exaggerate the length of several steps)

Step 5 Change of Place Left to Right

One boy can have fun with two girls in Jive

More Cha Cha Cha

Introduction

Here is an absolutely universal dance suitable for small floors, big floors, beginners and advanced dancers. You can be smart, sophisticated and sedate while cha cha cha'ing, or you can let your hair down and really give it a whirl.

In the **First Steps** chapter the basic steps were introduced, now it is time to expand your repertoire. If you have not mastered the basic movement perhaps you should check up on it again, then try this exciting new figure:

The Lady's Solo Right Turn
(Sometimes called the under arm turn)

Man's Steps

1.	*Left foot forward.*	*Step*
2.	*Right foot remains in place but weight is taken back on to it.*	*Step*
3.	*Left foot is placed close to right foot - say about 15 centimetres (six inches) away - weight is taken on to left foot when in position. Pull lady towards you slightly.*	*cha*
4.	*Right foot moves towards left foot and weight is taken on to it. Start lifting left hand, still holding lady's hand.*	*cha*
5.	*Left foot remains in place but weight is taken on to it. Man's left hand is now above head height and continues to rise, lady is going to turn under the arch formed by the joined man's left and lady's right hand. It is important not to grip the lady's hand too firmly - it will prevent her from making the turn if he does so.*	*Cha*
6.	*Right foot back, left hand is now raised well clear of lady's head and starts to make a small circle in a clockwise direction, holding the lady's hand loosely and allowing it to turn. The man is, as it were, stirring a pudding and making the lady turn quite strongly to her right.*	*Step*
7.	*Left foot remains in place but weight is taken forward on to it - by now the lady will have her back towards the man.*	*Step*
8.	*Right foot a small step to side, lady continues her turn.*	*cha*
9.	*Left foot half closes to right foot, lady still turning.*	*cha*
10.	*Right foot a small step to side, lady now facing man again and man lowering left hand back to starting position.*	*Cha*

More Cha Cha Cha

Lady's Steps

1.	Right foot back.	Step
2.	Left foot remains in place but weight is taken forward on to it.	Step
3.	Right foot a small step forward towards partner.	cha
4.	Left foot half closes to right foot.	cha
5.	Right foot a small step forward, preparing to turn to right.	Cha
6.	Left foot a small step to side, having turned strongly to right.	Step
7.	Right foot remains in place and lady continues turning - her back will be roughly towards partner at this point.	Step
8.	Left foot a small step to side, still turning so that lady's right side is now towards her partner.	cha
9.	Right foot half closes to left foot, still turning to right.	cha
10.	Left foot a small step to side, still turning to right to complete turn, now facing man again. Man regains hold as at start of figure.	Cha

This figure can be danced after the basic movement taught in the **First Steps** chapter. There is little difficulty in joining figures together in cha cha cha: all those given in this book can be taken after any other figure and they can be joined together in any sequence. There is an exception in the chasses given as an exercise in the **First Steps** chapter: they are not proper figures but merely building bricks from which figures are made.

Step 6 Lady's Right Turn

More Cha Cha Cha

The Fall-away Group
(Often called the hand to hand)

In this group the man changes from holding the lady's right hand in his left to holding her left hand in his right and then back to the starting hold again.

Man's Steps

Dance the basic movement as described in the first lesson but as steps 8,9 and 10 (a cha cha chasse) are taken, release hold of your partner from right hand and take hold of her left hand in your right hand. At this stage you will be holding both lady's hands in both your hands with hands held forward from the sides of the body so that there is, say, sixty centimetres (two feet) between the partners. As man the weight will be on the right foot. Then:

1.	*Left foot back a small step, releasing hold of lady's right hand from your left and having turned to left so that step can be taken back side by side with partner, who is also stepping back.*	*Step*
2.	*Right foot remains in place but weight is taken forward on to it, body starts to turn to right.*	*Step*
3.	*Left foot side a small step, turning to right - now nearly facing partner.*	*cha*
4.	*Right foot half closes to left foot, facing partner and taking hold of lady's right hand in your left hand so that you are again holding both partner's hands in yours.*	*cha*
5.	*Left foot a small step to side.*	*Cha*
6.	*Right foot a small step back, releasing hold of lady's left hand from your right and having turned to right so that step can be taken back side by side with partner who is also stepping back.*	*Step*
7.	*Left foot remains in place but weight is taken forward on to it, body starts to turn to left.*	*Step*
8.	*Right foot a small step to side, turning to left - now nearly facing partner.*	*cha*
9.	*Left foot half closes to right foot, facing partner and taking hold of lady's left hand in your right hand so that you are again holding both partner's hands in yours.*	*cha*
10.	*Right foot a small step to side, hold with both hands can be retained so that the whole figure can be repeated, or on this step the normal cha cha cha hold can be regained.*	*Cha*

Lady's Steps

1.	*Right foot back a small step, releasing hold of man's left hand from your right and having turned to right so that*

step can be taken back side by side with partner, who
is also stepping back.   Step

2. Left foot remains in place but weight is taken forward
   on to it, body starts to turn to left.   Step

3. Right foot side a small step to side, turning to left -
   now nearly facing partner.   cha

4. Left foot half closes to right foot, facing partner
   and taking hold of man's left hand in your right
   hand so that you are holding both partner's hands.   cha

5. Right foot a small step to side.   Cha

6. Left foot a small step back, releasing hold of
   man's right hand from your left and having turned
   to left so that step can be taken back side by side
   with partner who is also stepping back.   Step

7. Right foot remains in place but weight is taken
   forward on to it, body starts to turn to right.   Step

8. Left foot a small step to side, turning to right - now
   nearly facing partner.   cha

9. Right foot half closes to left foot, facing partner
   and taking hold of man's right hand in your left
   hand so that you are holding both partner's hands.   cha

10. Left foot a small step to side.   Cha

Cha Cha Cha

MAN and LADY

Fall-away group, the steps on the right are 1-5 inclusive while the steps on the left are 6-10 inclusive. The foot patterns are shown this way to avoid superimposition of the patterns.

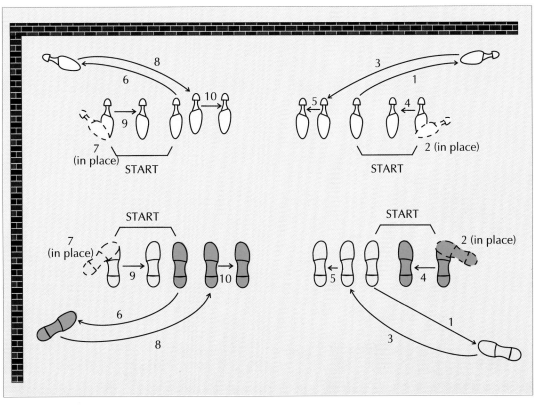

More Cha Cha Cha

New York Group
(This group's technical name is 'check from open promenade position')

Man's Steps
(Start facing wall, in open hold)

(See diagram on page 73 for steps 1-10)

1.	Left foot forward - not a long step.	*Step*
2.	Right foot remains in place, but weight is taken back on to it.	*Step*
3.	Left foot a small step to side.	*cha*
4.	Right foot half closes to left foot, starting to turn body to left and to turn lady to her right.	*cha*
5.	Left foot a small step to side, turning left side of body further away from partner and turning partner further to her right by pushing forward a little with left hand - couple are now in promenade position.	*Cha*
6.	Right foot a small step forward in promenade position, partner stepping forward in same direction - man and lady now facing line of dance approximately.	*Step*
7.	Left foot remains in place but weight is taken back on to it, body starts to turn to right towards partner.	*Step*
8.	Right foot a small step to side, man having first turned to right to face partner and taking right hand from partner's side, that is releasing hold with right hand.	*cha*
9.	Left foot half closes to right foot, man still turning right. The natural action of man's left hand when following the man's turn will turn the lady to her left. Man holds lady's right hand in his left.	*cha*
10.	Right foot a small step to side, man continuing his turn to right. Lady will continue turning to her left and both partners will be facing nearly in the same direction, man's left side will be towards lady's right side, and man and lady will have their backs to line of dance.	*Cha*
11.	Left foot forward a small step, lady also stepping forward (with her right foot). The nearest wall is on both man's and lady's left side.	*Step*
12.	Right foot remains in place, but weight is taken back on to it.	*Step*
13.	Left foot a small step to side, man having first turned to left to face partner, the movement of man's left arm will cause lady to turn her right to face man. Man lifts right hand and takes hold of lady's left hand in it.	*cha*

14.	*Right foot half closes to left foot, man still turning to his left, and lady to her right.*	*cha*
15.	*Left foot a small step to side, letting go of lady's hand with left hand. Man is now holding lady's left hand in his right hand and both are facing towards line of dance.*	*Cha*
16.	*Right foot forward a small step, in side by side position with partner - both facing line of dance.*	*Step*
17.	*Left foot remains in place but weight is taken back on to it.*	*Step*
18.	*Right foot a small step to side having turned to right towards partner. Action of man's right arm in turn will cause lady to turn to her left towards partner.*	*cha*
19.	*Left foot half closes to right foot - now facing partner, take hold of partner's side and back again with right hand - normal hold.*	*cha*
20.	*Right foot a small step to side - now facing partner and back in normal hold.*	*Cha*

Note: *It is not essential that the holds change exactly at the points given - a step out will make little difference.*

Step 16 New York Group

More Cha Cha Cha

Lady's Steps
(Start backing wall)

1.	*Right foot back - not a long step.*	*Step*
2.	*Left foot remains in place, but weight is taken forward on to it.*	*Step*
3.	*Right foot a small step to side.*	*cha*
4.	*Left foot half closes to right foot, starting to turn body to right*	*cha*
5.	*Right foot a small step to side, turning right side of body further away from partner - now in promenade position.*	*Cha*
6.	*Left foot a small step forward in promenade position, partner stepping forward in same direction - man and lady now facing line of dance approximately.*	*Step*
7.	*Right foot remains in place but weight is taken back on to it, body starts to turn to left towards partner.*	*Step*
8.	*Left foot a small step to side, turning to left to face partner, man will release hold on lady's back and side with his right hand.*	*cha*
9.	*Right foot half closes to left foot, still turning body to left.*	*cha*
10.	*Left foot a small step to side, continuing turn so that lady and man are both facing nearly in the same direction. Lady's right and man's left sides will be towards each other.*	*Cha*
11.	*Right foot forward a small step.*	*Step*
12.	*Left foot remains in place, but weight is taken back on to it.*	*Step*
13.	*Right foot a small step to side, having first turned to right to face partner. Man will take hold of lady's left hand in his right.*	*cha*
14.	*Left foot half closes to right foot, still turning to right.*	*cha*
15.	*Right foot a small step to side - now facing in same direction as man, towards line of dance.*	*Cha*
16.	*Left foot forward a small step, in side by side position with partner both facing line of dance.*	*Step*
17.	*Right foot remains in place but weight is taken back on to it.*	*Step*
18.	*Left foot a small step to side having turned to left towards partner.*	*cha*

19. Right foot half closes to left foot - now facing partner - man will regain normal hold.   *cha*

20. Left foot a small step to side - now facing partner and back in normal hold.   *Cha*

The shortest version of this figure has been described - it is possible, having danced steps 1 to 15, to follow with steps 6 to 15 again before moving on to step 16.

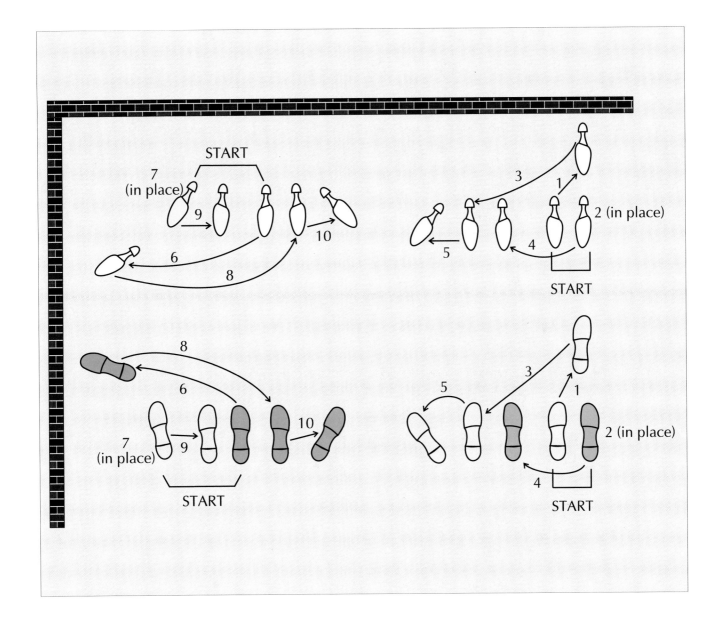

Cha Cha Cha   New York Group steps 1-10 only. Shown in two
MAN AND LADY   halves to avoid superimposition of the patterns.

Rumba

Introduction

This is the romantic dance of Cuba. Strictly speaking there are many forms of rumba and the name embraces traditional forms of dance and music such as son, danson, bolero and so on. Cha cha cha, mambo and salsa are recent derivations of rumba as it responded to the jazz influence. However, from the ballroom dance point of view rumba is the modern version of the traditional romantic dance.

Where cha cha cha is a lively, jaunty dance, rumba is subtle and sophisticated. It has a stately yet amorous style. While it has erotic undertones it is never blatant. It is the dance of lovers.

Many of the figures of cha cha cha and rumba are very similar. All the figures of the cha cha cha described so far in this book can also be danced in rumba by replacing the cha cha cha chasse with one step and subsequent hip action. The description of the rumba basic movement below, when compared with that already learnt for cha cha cha should make everything clear.

Rumba timing is more subtle than cha cha cha. The first actual step of the basic movement falls on the second beat of the bar of music and this can confuse. This arises because of the syncopation of the music. Most beginners instinctively listen to the phrasing of the melody and, as a result, want to move off on the first beat of the bar. To ensure the first step of the basic movement - and all subsequent figures - are taken on beat two of the bar, students should use the 'rhythm pick-up' now described.

Rhythm Pick-up

Man's Steps

1.	*Left foot a very small step to side.*	*One*
2.	*Replace weight onto right foot.*	*Two*
3.	*Close left foot to right foot.*	*Three*
4.	*Right foot to side - a very small step.*	*Four*
5.	*Leave weight on right foot and press right knee backwards forcing hips to right.*	*'Pause' (One)*

Lady's Steps

1.	*Right foot a very small step to side.*	*One*
2.	*Replace weight onto left foot.*	*Two*
3.	*Close right foot to left foot.*	*Three*
4.	*Left foot to side - a very small step.*	*Four*
5.	*Leave weight on left foot and press left knee backwards forcing hips to left.*	*'Pause' (One)*

It is this hip action, brought about by the straightening of the supporting leg on step 5 and the delay thus created, which give the rumba its special character. As the weight is taken on all rumba steps the leg should straighten fully, causing the hips to move sideways. The hip action is an essential part of the character of the dance and the action should be sideways and not rotary (as in the Hula hula) and should be from the waist downwards, leaving the shoulders steady.

Rumba

The Rumba hip action seen from side and front

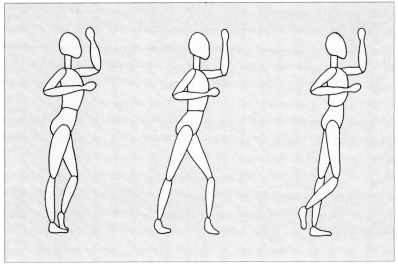

START   Left Foot moving forward........ to: END

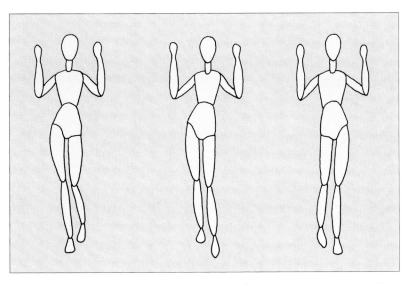

START   Left Foot moving to front   END

The rhythm pick up described can be followed by any normal figure, for example the Basic Movement as follows:

Rumba

Basic Movement

Man's Steps

1.	Left foot forward - not a long step.	Two
2.	Right foot remains in place but weight is taken back on to it.	Three
3.	Left foot a small step to side.	Four
4.	Leave weight on left foot and press left knee backwards, forcing hips to left.	'Pause' (One)
5.	Right foot back - not a long step.	Two
6.	Left foot remains in place but weight is taken forward on to it.	Three
7.	Right foot a small step to side.	Four
8.	Leave weight on right foot and press right knee backwards, forcing hips to right.	'Pause' (One)

Lady's Steps

1.	Right foot back - not a long step.	Two
2.	Left foot remains in place but weight is taken forward on to it.	Three
3.	Right foot a small step to side.	Four
4.	Leave weight on right foot and press right knee backwards, forcing hips to right.	'Pause' (One)
5.	Left foot forward - not a long step.	Two
6.	Right foot remains in place but weight is taken back on to it.	Three
7.	Left foot a small step to side.	Four
8.	Leave weight on left foot and press left knee backwards, forcing hips to left.	'Pause' (One)

Steps 3,4 and 7,8 of the above figure replace the cha cha cha chasse. In many of the simpler cha cha cha figures - and all included in this book - the cha cha cha chasses can be replaced by a step and hip action.

Foot diagrams have not been included because steps repeated in the same position, indicating just a weight change, can be confusing.

Introduction

In Chapter 2 the social foxtrot was introduced but the figures given do not give much variety. The following groups should now be learned to enlarge your dance 'vocabulary'.

Side Step

Man's Steps

1.	*Left foot to side.*	*Quick*
2.	*Right foot closes to left foot, keeping the weight on the left foot, that is, keep standing on the left foot.*	*Quick*
3.	*Right foot to side.*	*Quick*
4.	*Left foot closes to right foot, keeping the weight on the right foot.*	*Quick*
5.	*Left foot to side.*	*Quick*
6.	*Right foot closes to left foot, taking the weight on to the right foot.*	*Quick*
7.	*Left foot forward.*	*Slow*

Lady's Steps

1.	*Right foot to side.*	*Quick*
2.	*Left foot closes to right foot, keeping the weight on the right foot.*	*Quick*
3.	*Left foot to side.*	*Quick*
4.	*Right foot closes to left foot, keeping the weight on the left foot.*	*Quick*
5.	*Right foot to side.*	*Quick*
6.	*Left foot closes to right foot, taking the weight on to the left foot.*	*Quick*
7.	*Right foot back.*	*Slow*

The side step can follow the seventh step of the quarter turns and can be followed by the quarter turns or the natural turn.

Steps 1 to 6 of the side step can be repeated. If you relax and absorb the music a rhythmic action in the knees should become evident and you will feel you want to bend the supporting knee just a little on the second and fourth step of the side step. This is right and you should encourage the feeling.

More Social Foxtrot

Reverse Turn

The social foxtrot reverse turn is the second half of the quarter turns repeated (as the natural turn is the first half repeated).

Man's Steps
(After step 4 of the quarter turns)

1.	Right foot back starting to turn to left	Slow
2.	Left foot a small step to side, still turning to left	Quick
3.	Right foot closes to left foot, still turning to left	Quick
4.	Left foot forward - do not take too long a step and leave right foot in position	Slow
5.	Right foot back a few centimetres from position it is in , still turning to left	Slow
6.	Left foot a small step to side, still turning to left	Quick
7.	Right foot closes to left foot, still turning to left	Quick
8.	Left foot forward	Slow

The figure may be repeated as often as wished or it can be followed with the quarter turns or the right or natural turn. In the reverse turn the turn is not a strong one and at least four groups of four steps should be used to complete one full turn.

Lady's Steps

1.	Left foot forward, starting to turn to left.	Slow
2.	Right foot a small step to side, still turning to left.	Quick
3.	Left foot closes to right foot, still turning to left.	Quick
4.	Right foot back - do not take too long a step and leave left foot in position.	Slow
5.	Left foot forward a few centimetres from position it is in , still turning to left.	Slow
6.	Right foot a small step to side, still turning to left.	Quick
7.	Left foot closes to right foot, still turning to left.	Quick
8.	Right foot back.	Slow

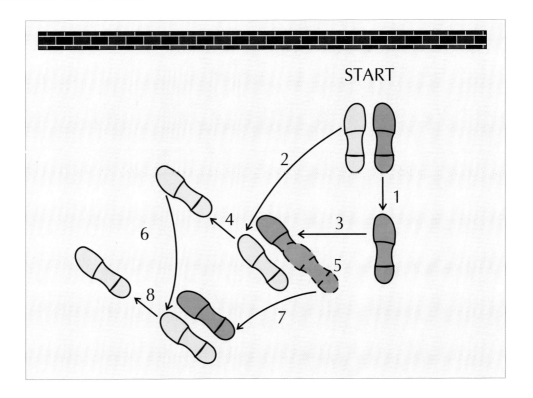

Social Foxtrot
MAN Reverse turn

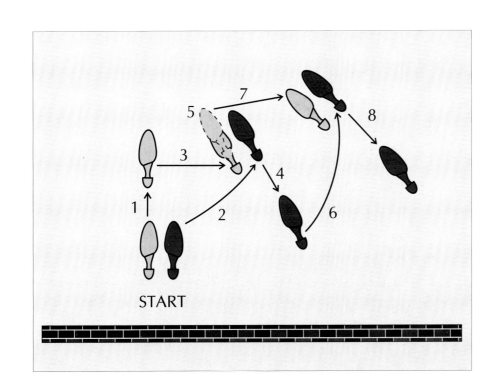

Social Foxtrot
LADY Reverse turn

Index